# SHELBY AMERICAN
## RACING HISTORY

Dave Friedman

Motorbooks International
Publishers & Wholesalers ®

First published in 1997 by Motorbooks International Publishers & Wholesalers, 729 Prospect Avenue, PO Box 1, Osceola, WI 54020-0001 USA

Motorbooks International books are also available at discounts in bulk quantity for industrial or sales-promotional use. For details write to Special Sales Manager at the Publisher's address

Library of Congress Cataloging-in-Publication Data Available

Friedman, Dave
Shelby American racing history / Dave Friedman.
p.   cm. — (Racing history)
Includes index.
ISBN 0-7603-0309-6 (pbk. : alk. paper)
1. Mustang automobile—History. 2. Ford GT40 automobile—History. 3. Cobra automobile—History. 4. Shelby American, Inc.—History. 5. Automobiles, Racing—United States—History. I. Title. II. Series.
TL215.M8F75  1997                                    97-21674
629.228—DC21

*On the front cover:* Allen Grant leads factory Cobra driver Lew Spencer into Riverside's Turn 7 during a 1963 endurance race run in conjunction with the *L.A. Times* Grand Prix.

*On the back cover: Top:* Publicity photo of R Model Mustangs under construction at the Shelby Imperial plant in mid-1965. *Bottom:* The Shelby King Cobras in the pit lane at Nassau in December 1963.

Printed in the United States of America

# Contents

# Preface

This is my last book on the Shelby American legacy; I promise. There are two very important reasons for this decision. First, this is the last of my best photography, and second, I've run out of usable stories. Of course, I have many stories that, for one reason or another, are not usable and those shall remain with me until such time as they can be published. All kidding aside, this book covers several aspects of the Shelby racing history that haven't been covered in my other books.

To provide you with some a background, I was the official photographer of Shelby American, both the company's racing effort and its production-car operation, from 1962 to 1967. This job gave me unlimited access to the Shelby operation and took me to some of the era's most spectacular race events, all around the world. It also helped me meet and become acquainted with some of the finest car builders, mechanics, racers—and characters—in all of racing history.

We will start off with some great photographs of the Cobras and Ford GT40s and then progress through some of the lesser-known Shelby projects, such as the Sunbeam Tiger and the Can-Am car, before winding up with the GT 350 Mustang and Trans-Am Mustang. It was with the Trans-Am Mustang that Shelby American's racing efforts terminated at the end of 1969.

I hope everyone will enjoy seeing some of the other projects that we at Shelby were involved in. Some of these projects were successful and some were not, but it just shows that we were only human and that we could accept our failures, too. Enjoy.

# Acknowledgments

I would like to acknowledge the help that I have received from the following people. Tim Parker gave me my start with Motorbooks. Michael Dregni and Mike Dapper taught me how to write captions, and Zack Miller has worked with me as the editor of this book. To all of them, a huge thank you. Susan Claudius corrected my grammatical errors and Maggie Moore, Alexis Callier helped me with some of the photographs. Thanks guys, you were great, as always. Once again, I also must thank Carroll Shelby. Without him there would have been no Shelby American, I would not have had that fantastic job, and there would have been none of these books.

—*Dave Friedman*

# The Cobra, Ford GT, and the Daytona Coupe

**This** is the toughest chapter in the book for me. Why? I've heard these stories from old cohorts so many times, and I've told these stories so many times to friends, race fans, and readers of my earlier Shelby books, that I find I may be saying little that's new about the Cobras, Daytona Coupes, and Ford GTs. Of course, I still have a number of photographs that are appearing here for the first time anywhere, and the accompanying caption material is new.

Most of the Cobra coupe photos shown here were taken early in the building process and have not been previously published. When I was preparing the photos-and-captions portion of *Daytona Cobra Coupes*, I discovered, with John and Paul Ohlsen's help, that the coupe in which a single-overhead-cam 427-cubic-inch engine was supposed to be placed actually received a 390-ci aluminum engine. Although this car never ran with anything but a 289-ci engine in it, the "what-ifs" persisted. I was able to trace the 390-ci engine lineage to and from that coupe, but I never could come up with a period

Exiting Turn 6 at Riverside in February 1963, Dave MacDonald leads Ken Miles during the modified race. Although Miles was a Shelby team driver, he was also allowed to race Otto Zipper's Porsche as long as it didn't interfere with his Cobra commitments, a common driver arrangement at that time. This was the last race in which the wire wheels were used on the factory Cobras. Wire wheels were extremely dangerous on high-powered, high-torque cars because the spokes could break or pull out of the hub, creating a very serious situation at high speeds. After this event, all of the Shelby team cars were equipped with Halibrand wheels.

John Ohlsen prepares to install the 390-cubic-inch engine in the modified Cobra coupe chassis in the background. It is truly unfortunate that this car never was able run in this configuration because it would have been something incredible to experience.

Dave MacDonald exits Turn 6 in his usual style. MacDonald won both the Saturday and Sunday races that weekend in February 1963. Ken Miles finished second, and this was the first of many one-two finishes that the Cobra team would experience before they ceased racing as a factory team in September 1965.

photo of the very rare 427-ci single-overhead-cam engine that was supposed to, but never did, get placed in the car. I never realized that, indeed, I had such a photo right under my nose. That photo is being published for the first time in this book. There are also some newly discovered stories and photos about the John Willment Cobra Coupe that raced in South Africa in 1964.

The Cobra roadster and Ford GT40 photographs in this book are also a collection of photos that have not been published before. Many of the Cobra photos shown in this book are of the privateer cars that helped to add so much to the racing history of Shelby American. Without them we would have never achieved much of the success that we enjoyed at

many of the major racing events from 1963 through 1965. The privateer teams were also responsible for many of the points that our team collected during our pursuit of the World Championship in 1964 and 1965. There are also some interesting early test and development photos here of the Ford GT40. Between the time that the first two GT40s arrived at Shelby American in December 1964, and the time that the cars appeared at Daytona in February 1965, I was the only one documenting their progress in photographs on a regular basis. Since none of these pictures appeared in my earlier book, *Shelby GT40*, published by Motorbooks International, and none of them were ever used in any of the English GT40 books, they are presented here for the first time.

Ken Miles (98) leads Dave MacDonald (198) into Riverside's famed Turn 6 in February 1963. By the time the race was over, the positions were reversed, and MacDonald had achieved the first of many race victories that Shelby American would experience over the next four years.

I also need to say a few words about the 427 Cobra photographs that appear here. I have always had a hard time trying to understand the mystique that certain people have tried to attach to these cars' supposed "illustrious racing history." The cold, hard facts are that, with the couple of exceptions illustrated here, most of these cars have no significant racing history at all. By the time these cars first appeared on the race track in early 1965, it was obvious to any novice spectator that, because of homologation problems, the new Cobras were not competitive with the modified cars against which they had to compete. By the time the 427 Cobra was homologated, it had been relegated to minor league club races, which hardly compared to racing with the big boys.

Let's not forget that the 427 Cobra never won a major professional or FIA race, and those are the races that counted and are remembered most. The 427 Cobra was a truly awesome street machine and worthy of most of the notoriety it achieved along

those lines, but it was hardly a top race car. I can well remember the many times that an unsuspecting customer came to Shelby American to collect a shiny new 427 Cobra, not knowing what he or she was in store for once they left the premises. I can also remember the bets among the Shelby American employees as to when, and in what condition, these cars would be returned to the shop.

The only two 427 Cobras that had any real racing history attached to them were a car raced by Skip Scott for Essex Wire and one driven by Tom Payne. These cars, particularly the Essex Wire car, ran in all or most of the major professional races in 1965. By contrast, the cars that ran in the SCCA events were running against little or no competition and, in most cases, were out for nothing but a Sunday drive.

Let's not forget that the Shelby American legacy was built on the exploits of the 289 Cobra and its glorious racing record. Without those cars there would have been no Shelby American.

As was the case in those days, many of the participants in the A and B production races also took part in the big-bore modified event. In February 1963, Dave MacDonald leads a multitude of cars through the Riverside esses into Turn 6. This was one of my favorite photographic spots at Riverside and this photo shows why. Behind MacDonald is Red Faris' (11) Corvette, Jay Hills' (81) Porsche Carrera, Paul Reinhart's (6) Corvette, Ronnie Bucknum's (31) Ol' Yeller, Ken Miles' (50) Porsche RS 61, Dick Guldstrand's (56) Corvette, Don Miline's (118) Corvette, and Pat Byran's (83) Ferrari Monza.

Two of the West Coast's best-known racers are shown racing through the parking lot and streets around Dodger Stadium in March 1963. Dave MacDonald and Dick Guldstrand (56) had many memorable West Coast races in the early sixties.

As they had at Riverside in February, the powerful Cobra team of Dave MacDonald (198) and Ken Miles (298) defeated a large and competitive field of A production cars at Dodger Stadium. Because the stadium is in a residential area, the Cobras were required to use a muffled exhaust system.

Carroll Shelby looks on as several spectators check the inner-workings of the factory Cobra racer at Pomona in July 1963.

Dave MacDonald was the weekend's big winner at the July 1963 Pomona race. MacDonald not only won both big-bore production races, he also won the modified race, beating Ken Miles' Dolphin-Porsche (50) by half a car length at the finish line.

Note the "high-tech fueling rig" being used by Tom Payne at the September 1963 Road America 500. This modern marvel of engineering excellence didn't contribute very much to Payne's effort since he was only able to finish 38th overall.

Even the boss gets in on the act. Carroll Shelby and Lew Spencer team up on a quick jack to help replace a tire at the 1963 Road America 500. Ken Miles (far left) watches the action.

Carroll Shelby looks to the heavens for divine guidance as the 1963 Bridgehampton 500 is about to start. Behind Shelby and out of the car (left), Ken Miles talks to Red Pierce, and Dan Gurney (in car) consults with Louie Unser (right), brother of racer Bobby Unser.

Bob Holbert congratulates Dan Gurney on his 1963 Bridgehampton 500 win. This was the first FIA manufacturer's win for the Shelby American Cobra.

15

Never let it be said that Cecil Bowman, head of the engine shop, did not use the most up-to-date technology in the assembly of the race team engines.

The heads for our 289-cubic-inch engines were given special attention.

Spare 289-cubic-inch engine blocks sit in the corner of the Shelby American engine shop.

Bob Bondurant (99), Dan Gurney (97), and Lew Spencer (98) crest Riverside's Turn 7 during the One Hour Enduro that preceded the 1963 Times Grand Prix. Bondurant won the race while Spencer finished third and Gurney finished fourth.

Look at this road ! This is typical of the type of road that the 1963 Tour de Corse rally was run on and the weather conditions were usually at their worst. This rally was seldom completed due to snowstorms, landslides, and heavy fog. No known record of how Schlesser and Vanson did in the rally exists, but a clue might be the fact that they went over a 60-foot cliff and destroyed their car the year before.

Jo Schlesser (right) and Patrick Vanson (left) stand by their Cobra prior to the start of the November 1963 Tour de Corse. This 24-hour rally, run in Corsica, was called the "Rallye of Ten Thousand Corners" for good reason.

PHOTO JUNIOR
34 AV. G. CLEMENCEAU
TEL. 723-56 NICE

Nassau provided a great opportunity to enjoy parties galore, great hotels, and first class food. Enjoying good food and good beer are (from left) Peyton Cramer (facing camera), Cecil Bowman, Dave MacDonald, Sherry MacDonald, Craig Lang, and Red Pierce.

Ken Miles (97) leads Mike Gammino's Ferrari GTO during the Nassau Trophy race. Miles did not finish and Gammino finished sixth overall.

Jim Hall's (65) Corvette Grand Sport leads Augie Pabst's (00) Lola Mk. 6-Chevrolet, Dick Thompson's (80) Corvette Grand Sport, Bob Holbert's (98) Cobra, John Everly's (106) Cobra, George Butler's (49) Cobra, and Mike Gammino's (23) Ferrari GTO at the start of the 1963 Nassau Tourist Trophy. Pabst won and none of the three Cobras finished.

I shot these photographs in early 1964 in order to compare the exterior of the first Cobra built (at right in front view; at left in rear view) with the latest 1964 model. Many changes are obvious such as the grille, wind wings, luggage rack, exhaust pipes, rag top, and deck latch.

Bob Holbert's (98) Cobra lines up for the start of the five-lap Texas Special Race. Next to Holbert is A. J. Foyt's (77) Scarab, and behind him is Charlie Kolb's (84) Harrison Special and J. Snyder's (79) Lister-Chevrolet. Holbert finished second while Kolb finished third. Foyt and Snyder did not finish.

This hard-top 289-cubic-inch Cobra was photographed at the 1964 New York Auto Show. As always, the Cobra display was one of the highlights of the show. Please note the small advertising photo card in front of the right front wheel. The rather interesting story about capturing that image follows next.

Ken Miles and Carroll Shelby celebrate Miles' win at the 1964 Bridgehampton 500. This was the team's second consecutive win at this FIA event.

This photograph was taken for and used in all of the initial 1964 advertising for the 289 Cobra. Pete Brock, with whom I worked very closely at that time, approached me one day with a most interesting and challenging job request. He needed me to shoot a picture of a Cobra sitting on a road, with a black background, and a light foreground for the advertising material that he was designing for our 1964 ad campaign and sales brochures. This would have been a relatively easy request if we had had access to a large photo studio where we could have worked under controlled lighting conditions, but we didn't have such an animal on our premises. After a lot of thought and some local location scouting, I came up with the following plan. My best friend, Dick Ableser, and I would drive the Cobra up to the Sepulveda tunnel early on a Sunday morning, hoping that traffic would be very light at that time. In 1963, Sepulveda Boulevard was still a major highway between the west side of Los Angeles and the San Fernando Valley and was heavily traveled. I had checked this spot out and I knew that if we parked the Cobra properly in front of the tunnel, we would achieve the requested black background and light foreground. When we arrived at the tunnel, the light was right and the Sunday morning traffic was extremely light. I made a U-turn in front of the tunnel and parked the Cobra in the middle of the road. Dick ran up the road and watched for oncoming traffic, and, most of all, the cops. I jumped out of the car, grabbed my camera, and shot the resulting picture. This was one of the most challenging jobs that I was given during my years at Shelby American, and we pulled it off. I somehow don't think that we could get away with such antics now.

Ken Miles' (98) 289 Cobra leads Tony Settember's (14) Webster Lotus 23B, Chuck Parsons' (187) Cooper-Chevrolet, and John Morton's (99) Lotus 23B out of Riverside's Turn 6 during the 1964 *L.A. Times* Grand Prix. Miles originally planned to debut his lightweight 390 Cobra in this race, but it was not completed in time. Miles lost a wheel and didn't complete the race.

A 1965 Cobra 289 sits in the Riverside pit area during a press showing of the entire Shelby line. This event took place before the USRRC race in May 1965.

Jean Ouellet's (83) Cobra leads a strong field of contenders away from the start of the Big Bore Sports Car Race that preceded the Player's Quebec Race at St. Jovite, Quebec, in September 1965. Following Ouellet is eventual race winner Tom Payne's (13) Cobra, Dan Gerber's (19) Cobra, John Cordts' (104) Corvette, and Jacques Duval's (58) Porsche 904. Gerber finished second overall, Cordts finished third overall, and Ouellet finished seventh overall.

Dan Gerber was one of the top Cobra independent drivers for several years. Gerber was also a member of the family that founded the well-known baby food business. The "Prune Mush" painting in the lower right-hand corner of this picture was done one night by Augie Pabst as a joke. The painting remained on the side of the car for the rest of the season.

Tom Payne (13) and Dan Gerber (19) had a successful weekend at St. Jovite in 1965. Payne won the Big Bore Production Race with Gerber a close second, and Payne also finished seventh overall in the Player's Quebec race while Gerber finished ninth.

The early laps of the 1965 Player's Quebec race illustrate the varied type of machinery that participated in these international professional races during the mid-sixties. With over and under 2-liter modified cars, plus over and under 2-liter GT cars competing in the same field, these races created some interesting and dangerous situations. They also created some very interesting final results. Jacques Duval's (58) Porsche 904 leads Tom Payne's (13) Cobra, Al Pease's (69) Alfa Romeo, and the rest of the field through Conner Corner early in the race.

Canadian driver Larry Cohen's (324) Cobra leads Jacques Duval during the production race at St. Jovite in September 1965. Cohen finished fifth overall.

By the time the Nassau races approached in December 1965, the 289-cubic-inch Cobra was about at the end of its competitive life. Dan Gerber's car was one of two Cobras that showed up that year at Nassau and his results were quite good. Gerber, leading Dick Holquist's (95) Ferrari 250LM, finished 18th in the Governor's Trophy Race and sixth in the Nassau Trophy Race.

Carroll Shelby (back to camera) watches as Ken Miles figures out the seating position he wants in the coupe. Pete Brock stands by (right) with a T-square and a tape measure while newly hired John Ohlsen (dark overalls at left) looks on. It was Ohlsen who was largely responsible for getting the coupe built, tested, and completed by the Daytona target date in mid-February 1964.

This was the first photograph taken when the Cobra coupe project was born in late October 1963.

Ron Moore works on completing the coupe buck.

John Ohlsen sits in the buck, demonstrating that a driver over 6 feet tall (such as Dan Gurney) could be seated comfortably in the coupe. Pete Brock (right) and his assistant, Ron Moore (left), look on.

Work progresses, as seen from the right rear side.

These next nine pictures are some of the unpublished photographs that I took during the Cobra coupe construction at Cal Metal Shaping in November 1963. Here, one of the Cal Metal employees fits the fender panels to the buck.

Clamps hold the body panels in place.

The front end begins to take shape. Note all of the completed body panels stacked in the background.

Pete Brock checks the fit of the top and right-side metal work as one of the Cal Metal workers forms a panel in the background.

By the time this photograph was taken, one could really get a feel for what the coupe would look like when it was completed.

These full-length photos show the progression of the aluminum panel construction. These pictures were taken over a period of several weeks.

This was the engine that was supposed to power the 427-cubic-inch Cobra coupe that was scheduled to run at Le Mans and Reims in June and July 1964. This 427-cubic-inch single overhead cam was originally built to compete in NASCAR and it was expected to debut at the February 1964 Daytona 500. Unfortunately for Ford, it was rejected by Bill France, the head of NASCAR, and never turned a wheel on the NASCAR circuit. This engine was then used successfully in the Ford drag racing program. It is obvious from this photograph that there would have been a serious problem trying to fit this engine into the Cobra coupe's chassis without extensive chassis and body modifications.

This is the 390-cubic-inch aluminum engine that was finally installed into the Cobra coupe.

This was the sleek Willment Cobra Coupe built by the Willment Racing team in 1964. This car had an extensive racing history both in England and South Africa and probably won more races than any other Cobra Coupe. The coupe sits in the pits at Kyalami in South Africa before the start of the nine-hour race on October 31, 1964.

The Willment Cobra Coupe (8) driven by Bob Olthoff and Jack Sears chases the eventual race-winning Ferrari 250LM driven by David Piper and Tony Maggs at Kyalami in 1964. The coupe finished fifth overall in the nine-hour race. It has always been rumored that Bob Olthoff attempted to set an African land speed record with this car but this is not true. Olthoff actually considered using this car for such an attempt but it never happened. Olthoff was going to attempt a high-speed run at the Capetown International Airport with this car, but the runways were too short and no other venue was available at that time for such an attempt.

This was the first Ford GT40 that was transferred to Shelby American in December 1964. The car sits in front of the TWA air freight office, waiting to be picked up by the Shelby American crew.

This was the second GT40 that was delivered to Shelby American. The car sits at LAX prior to being brought to the Venice race shop. The pilot (behind the car) of the plane that delivered the car can be seen checking out the cockpit.

Mechanics John Ohlsen (left) and Frank Lance (right) give the Ford GT40 a good cleaning on arrival at the shop. Race team painter "Tweety" (center) looks on. The cars were delivered to us with no cleanup by the John Wyer team after Nassau.

One of the first jobs that was undertaken by the Shelby crew before the first testing session was the installation of a Shelby-built engine. This, and a good cleanup, was about all that was done before the car was rushed to Riverside.

This is the Shelby American 289-cubic-inch engine that was in the Ford GT40 during the first testing session.

Jack Hoare makes some last-minute engine adjustments prior to the start of the first GT40 test session at Riverside.

Ken Miles (black sweatshirt at left) observes as Bob Bondurant prepares to take a few laps at Riverside. John Ohlsen is behind Miles and Frank Lance stands behind the passenger door. Miles was less than impressed with the GT40 as it was when he first tested the car at Riverside, and he decided to let Bondurant take over the driving chores for the rest of the day.

Bob Bondurant races down the long Riverside straight into Turn 9. Bondurant's first impressions of the GT40 were not as negative as those of Ken Miles.

Not much had changed on the car from this angle. The aluminum engine cooler lying under the transmission was one of the first improvements made in the engine compartment.

The aircraft fittings (seen in the engine compartment) were one of the first modifications done to the GT40s by the Shelby team. Many more changes were to come.

Several modifications took place on the front section of the car by the time we returned to Riverside for another test. Note the larger air vents that had been cut in the nose panel to enhance the poor radiator cooling. Look closely, and you can also see the air scoops that were added under the nose to increase cooling to the brakes.

The engines were immediately removed when the GT40s returned to the Venice shop after their victory at Daytona.

One of the most important undertakings after the Daytona race was the complete overhaul of the GT40 chassis. Shelby American elected to return the cars to California so that they could both be entirely rebuilt rather than keep the cars in Florida between the Daytona and Sebring races.

This was how the GT40 roadster appeared when it was first delivered to Shelby American in March 1965.

The Shelby-prepared
Scuderia Filipinetti GT40
heads for Le Mans.

The roadster sits on the
loading ramp prior to its
departure for France. The
larger radiator cooling
ducts cut in the front body
section are seen here.

This is the way the GT40 roadster
looked when it left Shelby American in
June 1965 bound for Le Mans. A
number of changes had been made to
the car during the three months that we
had the car, and a couple of those
modifications are seen here. The nose
configuration has been extensively
modified to increase cooling to the
brakes and radiator and also to help
improve the car's less-than-acceptable
aerodynamics. The rear body panel has
been widened to accept the Halibrand
wheels and wider tires.

The Shelby American Cobra 427 debuted at the Riverside USRRC race in May 1965. Since the car was not homologated, it had to run with the modified cars. Ken Miles' (98) Cobra 427 leads Jerry Titus' (76) Webster 2 Liter, and Jim Hall's (66) Chaparral 2. Hall won the race and Miles lasted 25 laps before departing with engine problems.

Lothar Motschenbacher (1) also debuted his 427 Cobra at the May 1965 Riverside USRRC race. Motschenbacher leads Bob Challman's (2) Lotus 30, Bob Montana's (15) Plymouth Special, and Chuck Parsons' (17) Lotus 30 into Turn 7. Motschenbacher retired his car after 21 laps with unknown problems.

Miles did not appear at the Laguna Seca USRRC race with the Shelby 427 Cobra, but Motschenbacher did, and he finished seventh overall against some of the top modified sports cars in the country.

Dick Thompson (91) battles Tony Settember's (36) Lotus 23B
for position in Laguna Seca's famous Turn 9 in October
1965. This spot was one of the best photographic areas on
the West Coast. Thompson finished 10th overall.

Dick Thompson's (91) 427 Cobra leads Miles Gupton's (75)
Platypus, Tony Settember's (36) Lotus 23B, and Rick Muther's
(11) Lola T70 into Turn 1 during the October 1965 Monterey
Grand Prix at Laguna Seca. Thompson qualified 20th on the
grid.

There is no question that the one 427 Cobra with a real race record was this one, raced by Skip Scott and others during the 1965 USRRC and West Coast Pro Series season. At the Road America 500 in September 1965, Dick Thompson and Ed Lowther finished third overall.

A pit stop at the Road America 500. This car's race debut was at the Pensacola USRRC race on April 11, 1965, making it the first 427 Cobra to compete in a major race.

Dick Thompson finished 15th overall in the October 1965 *L.A. Times* Grand Prix at Riverside.

Ed Lowther drove the Essex Wire Cobra 427 at the Las Vegas Stardust Grand Prix in November 1965. Lowther qualified 19th in a field of 30 contenders.

Dick Thompson crests the hill at Riverside's Turn 7. Behind Thompson is the Scarab of Augie Pabst.

Ed Lowther might have finished higher than his 11th place overall in Las Vegas if he hadn't had to pit for fuel. Competing against Chaparrals, Lolas, and McLarens was no easy matter.

Dick Thompson was back in the Essex Wire Cobra at Nassau in December 1965. In typical Cobra Nassau luck, the car failed to finish either the Governor's Trophy or the Nassau Trophy races. Note the movie camera attached to the roll bar. I wonder if that film still exists today.

This 427 Cobra, driven by Bob Grossman and Ed Lowther, finished 10th overall in the 1966 Sebring 12 Hour race.

Since the 427 Cobra was created too late to compete in the FIA GT category, it had to compete in a class in which it was completely outmanned. The Sports Car class featured such entries as Porsche 906s, Ford Mk. IIs, Chaparrals, and Ferraris. Well, you get the idea.

The team of John
Bentley, H. Byrne, and
Arthur Latta finished
22nd overall at Sebring
in 1966 in this 427
Cobra.

George Eaton had just finished second overall in the Production Sports Car race that preceded the 1966 Player's 200, run at Mosport, when he stopped to pick up Eppie Wietzes, whose Mustang (below) had just broken a wheel. Believe it or not, the car that beat the 427 Cobra that day was an MGB.

A mixed and interesting field started the Player's 200 in June 1966. Nat Adams' (169) Cooper Ford leads Tom Payne's (13) 427 Cobra, Eitel Maier's (113) Lotus 23B, Rudy Bartling's (145) Porsche RS61, and David Greenblatt's (411) Ferrari 250LM early in the race.

Tom Payne's (13) 427 Cobra leads George Fejer's (88) Chinook and Rick Muther's (45) McLaren during the first heat of the Player's 200 in June 1966. Payne, wearing his famous coat and tie, finished 10th overall in the final standings.

In 1966, the Nassau Tourist Trophy and the Governor's Trophy races were combined due to lack of entries for the Tourist Trophy race. Bob Grossman finished sixth overall and third in GT.

A strong, international field of cars started the Nassau Trophy Race in December 1966. Skip Scott's (92) McLaren leads the field away from the Le Mans start. Behind Scott, the pack includes Bob Grossman's (6) Cobra 427, Mark Donohue's (7) Lola T70, Buck Fulp's (26) Lola T70, Peter Revson's (91) McLaren, and Kenneth Duclos' (34) Cicada Special. Donohue won the race and Grossman finished 13th overall. By the end of the 1966 season the 427 Cobra had run its course and was relegated to the minor league club racing circuit.

# ②　The Sunbeam Tiger

The Sunbeam Tiger project was actually the idea of Ian Garrad, who in 1964 was the West Coast manager of Rootes Motors. Garrad, an astute Englishman, had been in North America since 1951 and had a keen sense of what the sports car enthusiast in the United States demanded in the way of a car's performance.

The Sunbeam Alpine had been a reasonably successful seller in North America, but the big knock on the car was that it was underpowered. Garrad realized that wins on the race track were a sports car's best advertising. Acting independently, he set out to build a prototype V-8-powered Alpine. One of Garrad's big problems was deciding which V-8 would fit into the Sunbeam chassis with minimal modification. West Coast racing mechanic Doane Spencer recommended that Garrad use the 260-cubic-inch Ford's engine, as Carroll Shelby had in his early Cobras.

Spencer had hoped to land the job of building the prototype, but that deal went to Shelby American. This project came to us at a time when our small Venice race shop was already overcrowded, not because Shelby never turned down work, but because we had too many team and customer cars to care for and not enough work space or bodies. This overcrowding was the primary reason that we moved to the airport in the spring of 1965. Garrad wanted Shelby to build two prototypes, one for the street and one for the track, but the time frame was too narrow for Shelby to handle the construction of both cars.

Lew Spencer's first race in the Tiger came shortly after a heavy rainstorm. This certainly didn't help Spencer overcome the ill-handling characteristics of the car. Note the oil cooler that has been mounted under the front bodywork of the car.

Donn Allen works on the brake modifications and brake air scoops as the car is readied for the installation of the engine. Note the Halibrand wheel and tire leaning against the Alpine's door. These were the wheels and tires that were about to be mounted on the Tiger for its first race at Tucson.

A red Sunbeam Alpine sits in our Venice shop in the fall of 1963 awaiting a Ford 260-cubic-inch engine and other modifications that will turn it into the first Sunbeam Tiger racing car.

By the time this picture was taken, the battery had been placed in the trunk, the racing-style windscreen had been installed, and the wider tires and Halibrand wheels were being fitted. Several publications have indicated that this car was white when it was delivered to our shop. Obviously, someone was color blind or badly misinformed.

Although Ken Miles worked for Shelby American at the time, he still maintained a small workshop of his own, where he did some outside work. Miles was given the task of building the first Sunbeam Tiger street car and Shelby built the first race car. After much modification, the first race car made its debut at the SCCA divisional race run at Tucson in early April 1964. The driver was the very capable Lew Spencer, who had years of experience racing production sports cars. His performance at Tucson proved that the Tiger had possibilities but that a lot of work was needed to make the car a winner. The biggest problem with the Tiger was that it tended to swap ends without warning at the most inopportune times. This, of course, did little for the driver's confidence in the car. The problem—never cured by the Shelby crew—was likely caused by too much horsepower installed in a too-short chassis.

In the June 1964 Willow Springs SCCA divisional race, Spencer managed to win the Sunbeam Tiger's first B Production race, but at the Laguna Seca USRRC (United States Road Racing Championship)

race several weeks later he crashed heavily on the fastest part of the circuit, severely injuring his back. Spencer never set foot in the car again.

The last time the Tiger was raced as a Shelby American entry, Ken Miles drove the car at the Badger 200, which was a prelude to the more-famous Road America 500 held every September. Miles finished second overall to Dan Gerber's A Production Cobra and won the B Production Class.

Shelby's commitment to the 1965 World GT Championship, the Ford GT, and the GT 350 Mustang dictated that the Tiger development program be turned over to someone who had the time to properly pursue it. That person turned out to be Doane Spencer of Hollywood Sports Cars, who turned the Tiger into a reasonably decent race car. But many people still wonder what would have happened had Shelby American had the time and manpower to pursue the Tiger project properly.

The Sunbeam Tiger sits on one of the airport runways that was used to stage the Tucson SCCA Divisional event in April 1964. Shelby American mechanics John Morton (left) and Ted Sutton look on as driver Lew Spencer warms the car up before the first practice session. The Shelby American pickup truck and trailer, far right, indicates that the Tiger had just been unloaded after completing its trip from the California race shop.

Ian Garrad (left) and Doane Spencer were two of the key players in the Tiger saga. Garrad was the West Coast manager for Rootes Motors and the one who conceived the possibility of putting an American V-8 in the Sunbeam chassis in the first place. Spencer, competition manager for Hollywood Sports Cars, had built a number of very successful West Coast championship production sports cars for Ronnie Bucknum and Jim Adams. He would take over the Tiger program after Shelby ran out of time and space for it.

One of the obvious modifications done to the Tiger by the Shelby race shop was this hood scoop. The scoop forced more air into the radiator of the Ford engine and helped prevent possible overheating problems.

Ted Sutton (left) makes an engine adjustment as John Morton and Lew Spencer (right) look on.

This photograph of Lew Spencer at speed in the Tiger at Tucson became one of the best-known of all of the early Tiger pictures. This photograph was used in all of the early advertising and publicity pieces.

The Tiger sits in the pits as one of the team mechanics (under the car) checks the rear end.

Lew Spencer pulls away from Doug Hooper's Corvette during the Sunday B Production race at Tucson. Spencer's chance for victory was spoiled when he had tire problems early in the race. Although the best he could do was finish 12th overall, Spencer had proved that the possibilities were there.

Lew Spencer takes one his several off-course excursions during the Tucson race weekend. Most of the spins were caused by too much power being stuffed in too short a wheelbase.

Upon its return from Tucson, the Sunbeam Tiger underwent a complete overhaul at the Shelby race shop in Venice, California.

During an early practice session at Willow Springs, Lew Spencer decided to explore the possibilities of finding a rattlesnake in the desert sun. He failed in this endeavor but succeeded in the more important business at hand.

Willow Springs provided the Sunbeam Tiger with its first production sports car victory. This photograph of Lew Spencer appeared in numerous magazine ads.

Lew Spencer drifts out of Laguna Seca's Turn 9 during the B Production race that preceded the USRRC race in May 1964.

Lew Spencer flat out through turn 2 the fastest part of the beautiful Laguna Seca circuit.

As Lew Spencer approached Turn 2, the Tiger left the circuit at high speed and climbed the dirt hill approaching the spectator area. Spencer can be seen still sitting in the car holding his neck as crew member Ted Sutton (far left) goes for help. This misadventure was just another in a series of wild spins and off-course excursions that were caused by the Tiger's serious handling problems. The short wheelbase of the Alpine chassis coupled with the power of the Ford engine made for a lethal handling package that convinced Spencer to return to racing the Cobras and leave the driving of the Tiger to someone else.

The Shelby Sunbeam
Tiger returned to the
track for the Badger
300 at Road America in
September 1964. Ken
Miles was the driver
and the Tiger finished
second overall and won
the B Production class.
Dan Gerber's Shelby
Cobra won the race
overall. Note the new
hood scoop.

Ken Miles appeared with another Tiger in the Three Hour Enduro for production cars that preceded the *L.A. Times* Grand Prix at Riverside in October 1964. Miles did not finish because of a blown engine on the ninth lap.

Ken Miles moves under the Corvette Stingray of Gibson Hufstader, who finished fifth overall.

Ken Miles leads the High Performance Motors' Shelby Cobra of Lew Spencer through Turn 7 during the early stages of the production race at Riverside in 1964. Miles failed to finish, while Spencer finished fifth overall. Spencer had led the race early on but had a long pit stop because of a broken oil line.

Shelby American's involvement in modified sports car racing actually began in early 1963 when driver-mechanic Dave MacDonald persuaded Carroll Shelby that building a modified sports car could become one of Shelby's better ideas. MacDonald and Shelby both felt that the team could be very competitive in the lucrative FIA and USAC West Coast Series that took place at Kent, Washington, and at Riverside and Laguna Seca in California. These races were run in the fall and drew full fields of international driving talent, along with record crowds of spectators.

These races also drew unprecedented press coverage in major newspapers and magazines worldwide, and, if the team was fortunate enough to win any of these events, itcould provide Shelby American with millions of dollars in free publicity.

It was decided that the basic Cooper Monaco chassis would be used, because the Cooper could be easily adapted to accommodate the 289-cubic-inch Ford engine. The first chassis shipped by Cooper Cars Ltd. arrived at Shelby American in the late summer, and Crew Chief Wally Peat immediately set to work readying the car—including considerable chassis modification—for testing at Riverside. The initial King Cobra test session was one of those very rare testing days when everything went right from the beginning, and the car's performance was absolutely flawless.

From the King Cobra's first race at Kent, Washington, in September 1963, it was evident that Shelby American had come up with another winner. Although overheating problems forced the two cars, driven by Bob Holbert and Dave MacDonald, from

This picture was taken after Dave MacDonald had won the two biggest professional sports car races in the world (the Times Grand Prix at Riverside and the Pacific Grand Prix at Laguna Seca) on successive weekends. Race Queen Marilyn Fox sits behind the wheel of MacDonald's King Cobra as Dave looks on.

The Shelby team cars sit in the pit lane at Nassau in December 1963. They should have stayed there.

The two King Cobras and Roger Penske's incredibly fast Cooper-Chevrolet (36) prepare to start the 1963 Texas Special five-lap race. Penske won the race while Holbert (98) finished second and MacDonald (97) finished fourth.

The only major race at Nassau in 1963 that both of the King Cobras participated in was the Nassau Trophy Race. Bob Holbert lasted only six laps before he went out with suspension problems.

Dave MacDonald (97) leads Uwe Beuhl's (75) Porsche RS 61 and Roger Penske's (36) Cooper-Chevrolet during the 1963 Nassau Trophy Race. On lap 27, MacDonald, like Holbert, had a major suspension failure. The Cooper's fragile suspension was no match for the rough Oakes Field circuit.

In December 1963, MacDonald's amazing luck ran out at Nassau, where the rough track conditions caused havoc with all of the Shelby entries. In spite of all of the success that the Shelby American team had achieved worldwide in the company's first full year of racing, Nassau always proved to be the one place where the team just could not get it right.

By the time race day arrived, Parnelli had sorted himself and the car out. By the end of the first lap, Jones was in second place and by the time lap three was completed, he had assumed the lead, which he maintained, in spite of losing his clutch on the 20th lap, to the end of the race. Jones is shown here leading Shelby teammate Richie Ginther through Turn 7. Note the nose damage to Jones' car that occurred during a little qualifying race altercation with Jerry Grant's Lotus 19. Richie Ginther finished seventh overall and Parnelli Jones became the second winner of the Times Grand Prix in as many years for Shelby American. The Shelby King Cobra was the first marque to win this prestigious race two years in a row.

Parnelli Jones picked the 1964 *L.A. Times* Grand Prix to make his sports car racing debut and he did it in spectacular fashion. Driving a Shelby American King Cobra, Jones, who had no previous testing or practice time in the car prior to the start of official practice, was one of the fastest drivers on the course. "Since I was completely unfamiliar with the car and I didn't really have time to sort it out, I had to drive it as hard as I could and see how far I could push it," Parnelli told me not too long ago. Jones' practice sessions resulted in several wild off-course excursions like this one at Turn 7.

the race, the cars set several track records. By the time that the race series moved to Riverside for the *Los Angeles Times* Grand Prix, the team was ready for a maximum effort in front of a record hometown crowd.

Holbert retired with overheating problems early in the Riverside race, but MacDonald went on to a record-setting win, lapping the entire international field. A week later, MacDonald won the Pacific Grand Prix at Laguna Seca, but it was not an easy chore. Holbert set a new track record and led the race until he collided with a back marker while lapping him. MacDonald had endured a terrible weekend leading up to the race. During qualifying, his engine blew, and he wasn't able to post a qualifying time.

During the Sunday morning warm-up, he was involved in a crash that left his car with a bent frame. For a while it wasn't known if MacDonald could even start the race, let alone have a chance to win.

Starting in the back of the pack—with a faulty transmission—MacDonald worked his way through the field to achieve his second record-setting win in as many weeks. These two wins created more exposure for Shelby American, and Ford than we could have ever imagined and catapaulted a relatively unknown driver to international fame.

In late December, the Shelby crew traveled to Nassau, but as always, the team was snake bit there and none of the cars were competitive. The suspension and the engines of the Shelby cars never seemed to last long on the very rough Oakes Field circuit (an abandoned airfield) and, unbelievably in comparison to the team's overall race record, no Shelby car ever had a podium finish at Nassau. The racing often played second fiddle to the round of outstanding parties and social events that were always planned for the Nassau Speed Week. All the drivers and crews always looked forward to Nassau because they considered it a paid vacation. The race week was run under very liberal FIA rules, with promoter Sherman "Red" Crise pretty much making up his own rules as to who ran in what classes.

In 1964, MacDonald won a couple of USRRC races in the King Cobra before he was killed at Indianapolis that year. MacDonald was loved by all the other Shelby American employees, which was why there was such an incredible outpouring of grief after his death. The reason for this special relationship was that Dave worked daily in our race shop as a mechanic, in addition to his team driving chores. Everyone knew him and liked him, and he was part of the close brotherhood that existed at the Venice facility.

Even with MacDonald's wins, the handwriting was on the wall as the more advanced Chaparrals began to dominate the sports car series and the new McLaren began to appear at the fall races. Parnelli Jones managed to win the *Times* Grand Prix for Shelby American, but by the end of the year, the King Cobra was relegated to the boneyard.

By the time the 1965 season rolled around, the Shelby American team was consumed with two major projects: winning the world manufacturer's championship and making the Ford GT a winner. A half-hearted effort to construct a Group Seven sports car for the 1965 pro season was soon scrapped when it was found that the car would never be in the same league as the Chaparrals, McLarens, or the Lolas. No further attempt at a Group Seven car was made until the ill-fated, Len Terry–constructed King Cobra appeared at *Times* Grand Prix in October 1967. This car, driven by Jerry Titus, was ill-conceived from the beginning and was in no way competitive with the front-running McLarens, Lolas, and Chaparrals. It was a

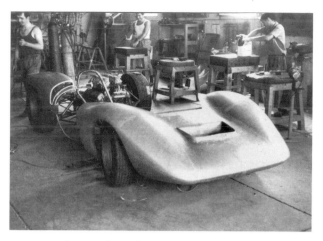

It was obvious that after the Pacific Grand Prix in October 1964, the King Cobra had achieved about as much as it could and, with the advent of the Chaparral 2 and the new McLaren M1A, it was a relic of the past. In late 1964 Pete Brock conceived the idea of building a new Shelby American sports racer to compete in the 1965 professional series. After some discussion, Brock convinced Shelby to use his Lang-Cooper body design and build the car in conjunction with DeTomaso at the Fantuzzi shop in Modena, Italy. By the time construction of the car finally commenced, it, like the earlier King Cobra, was out of date and it was soon realized that it would not be competitive with the new Lolas, McLarens, and Chaparrals that were dominating the professional sports car racing scene at the time. The project was therefore scrapped before construction of the car was completed. It is rumored that the car was eventually completed and actually ran, unsuccessfully, in a race in Italy.

disaster, running a total of just three laps in the two races in which it appeared. The car suffered numerous suspension and engine problems that were never worked out, because Ford and Shelby never considered the project a top priority.

In 1966 and 1967, Shelby American had been so busy with the Ford Mk. II and Mk. IV programs that the time needed to develop a competitive Can-Am car just wasn't there, in spite of the many high-quality, multitalented people working for Shelby at the time.

In 1968, the Shelby racing team made a commitment to run the entire Can-Am series, but Ford's lack of interest in developing a competitive racing engine doomed the project from the beginning. Peter Revson—an outstanding driver who in 1971 would

Shelby American did not build a car for the 1966 Can-Am season, but the company finally got one together for the last two races of the 1967 Can-Am. The whole effort was a huge mistake from the very beginning. The car, dubbed King Cobra, was designed by Len Terry and the chassis was built in England. After numerous delays, the chassis finally arrived at the Shelby facility (a converted airport hangar) on Imperial Boulevard. Sitting in the chassis is mechanic Mark Popov-Dadiani while John Collins (far left), Phil Remington, Len Terry, and Red Pierce look on. Note all of the 1967 Shelby GT 350 and GT 500 Mustangs awaiting delivery in the background.

become the first American to win the Can-Am Championship—drove a McLaren M6B prepped by Shelby and running a Ford engine in all six of the events. The best finish he could achieve, however, was a fourth place in the season's first race at Road America.

The M6B was a very good car, and it always ran near the front until it was sidelined by various (mostly engine) problems. Unfortunately, Ford did little or nothing to support any of the Can-Am teams using its engines. After considerable frustration, most teams switched to Chevrolet engines. Following the final race at Las Vegas and one at Fuji raceway in Japan, at the end of the 1968 season, the Shelby team packed it in. No Shelby American entry was ever seen again at a professional sports car race.

The engine that was to power the new King Cobra was a 351-cubic-inch Ford. Several different engine configurations (such as 325 cubic inch) were tried, but the 351-cubic-inch engine was the best option at the time. By this time Ford had fallen way behind Chevrolet in the art of Can-Am engine development.

The King Cobra's aluminum monocoque is plainly visible in this picture. The extremely long nose contains the radiator, which lies horizontally. This, however, did not work, and the radiator was relocated to the rear of the car when the original placement failed to adequately cool the engine. Note the single coil spring that is mounted just behind the nose. This was part of the suspension and a similar setup was mounted in the rear of the car. When one of the springs popped out of the car during a Riverside test session, this idea was scrapped in favor of the more conventional method.

Jerry Titus was chosen to drive the King Cobra in the 1967 Can-Am series. Most of the crew felt that a better choice could have been made because, as good as he was in a Trans-Am car, Jerry lacked the experience, finesse, and know-how to properly evaluate a more powerful Can-Am car. He's seen testing here at Riverside.

The King Cobra sits in the Shelby shop prior to going to Riverside for testing.

Jerry Titus heads down the front straight at Riverside during an August 1967 test session. Smoke is evident at the rear of the car. The test report from that day indicates that Titus was having a number of problems with the car. Among the problems were pushing in the fast corners, slow steering, and an engine that felt flat.

Typical of the many problems that the car encountered during the August 1967 Riverside testing sessions was this terminal loss of oil pressure on the front straight. At this time, a 325-cubic-inch Ford engine was being used for test evaluation, while the Shelby crew developed a 351-cubic-inch Ford engine with Gurney Weslake heads for the Can-Am events.

Mark Popov-Dadiani makes an adjustment at Riverside. Riverside was a second home to everyone involved with the Shelby race team. It was approximately 75 miles from the shop and we spent many days making round-trips to that track. A number of teams used Riverside to test, and I'm sure that Shelby got a special deal because we were out there, it seemed, daily. The Shelby Driving School also ran at Riverside almost daily.

Under the watchful eye of Phil Remington (far right), Mark Popov-Dadiani (right) and John Collins (left) prepare to remove the rear body section in order to make adjustments. Jerry Titus can be seen behind Collins while Len Terry stands between Popov-Dadiani and Remington. The holes that were originally cut in the front of the bodywork were grossly inadequate for cooling, and the entire front and rear sections were extensively modified before the car appeared at the Riverside Can-Am in October 1967.

Jerry Titus doesn't look happy as he sits in the cockpit of the King Cobra during Can-Am practice. Crew members Jim O'Leary, John Collins, Carroll Smith, Phil Remington, and Carroll Shelby look on.

Jerry Titus looks happier after qualifying 13th in a field of 39 starters.

The completely reworked bodywork is evident while the car sits in the pits during practice for the Riverside Can-Am. Note the tabs on the front body panel and the spoiler on the rear body panel to help improve the handling. Also note all of the new holes cut in the body to improve cooling. Jerry Titus talks to Phil Remington and Carroll Smith while John Collins and Mark Popov-Dadiani stand at the right rear of the car. Standing behind Remington and Smith are Jim O'Leary and well-known engine builder Ryan Falconer.

The initial race for the King Cobra and Jerry Titus ended after just three laps. A broken fuel pump was the cause for the car's departure from the race. Two weeks later, at Las Vegas, the car failed to start the race due to suspension failure and was never seen again.

In 1968, the Shelby team ran a Lola T70 in the first three USRRC events with Peter Revson as the driver. Using a Ford 377-cubic-inch engine with Gurney Weslake heads, Revson qualified on the pole for the season's first race in Mexico City and finished third after an early-lap pit stop.

The Can-Am season started at Road America on September 1, 1968, and the Shelby team arrived with a new McLaren M6B powered by a Ford 427-cubic-inch aluminum engine. Peter Revson qualified seventh after having minor problems during practice.

Seen here at Riverside, Revson qualified fourth but started third after Jim Hall's Chaparral 2G was withdrawn before the start of the race. Revson was running third when he pitted on the 23rd lap with a blown engine. When the series moved to Kent, Washington, in June, another Shelby Lola appeared with a 427-cubic-inch Ford aluminum, fuel-injected engine with Revson driving. In qualifying, Revson lowered the track record by two full seconds and qualified for the pole. When the race started, Revson was in second place until the engine let go on the second lap. It was found that the engine that ran in Revson's car that day was full of aluminum swarf and steel chips. After the Kent race, Shelby withdrew the Lola from the USRRC series and it was used to test various engine configurations for the upcoming Can-Am schedule. It is interesting to note that the Shelby Lola was the only car capable of running with, or possibly beating, the Mark Donohue/Roger Penske McLaren M8A that won the series championship that year.

The 1968 Road American Can-Am started under less than terrific conditions and the weather did not improve during the race. Peter Revson's (52) McLaren M6B leads Pedro Rodriguez' (2) Ferrari 330 P4, Charlie Hayes' (25) McKee Mk. 7, Jerry Hansen's (44) McLaren M6A, and Ronnie Bucknum's (32) Lola T70 Mk. 3B during the parade lap. You will notice that, even at slow speed, the bad weather conditions made for some serious vision problems.

Peter Revson leads George Eaton's (98) McLaren M1C as weather conditions worsen at Road America in 1968. In spite of the conditions, Revson would finish fourth overall and this would be his best finish of the year.

Peter Revson is running flat out at Bridgehampton in September 1968. Revson qualified third overall.

Several thousand horsepower and lots of incredible ground-shaking noise was what accompanied this field of legendary cars and drivers as they raced through Hansgen Corner on the first lap of the 1968 Bridgehampton Can-Am. Denis Hulme's (5) McLaren M8A leads Peter Revson's (52) McLaren M6B, Mark Donohue's (6) McLaren M6B, Dan Gurney's (48) McEagle, Jim Hall's (66) Chaparral 2G, Mario Andretti's (21) Lola T70 Mk. 3B, Lothar Motschenbacher's (11) McLaren M6B, John Surtees' (7) Lola T160, and Chuck Parsons' (10) Lola T160 toward the Millstone Turn.

The 1968 Can-Am race at Laguna Seca was run under some of the worst weather conditions ever seen at the scenic Monterey, California, circuit. Since the qualifying session was held earlier in the week on a dry track, Revson qualified fourth overall behind Jim Hall, Denis Hulme, and Bruce McLaren. When Sunday morning dawned, the rain came pouring down and the track conditions became extremely dangerous, especially on the corkscrew. Peter Revson leads Jerry Entin's (12) Lola T70, Denis Hulme's (5) McLaren M8A, Mark Donohue's (6) McLaren M6B, and George Follmer's (34) Lola T70 Mk. 3B down a very slippery corkscrew.

Peter Revson laps George Eaton's (98) McLaren M1C and Stan Burnett's (64) Burnett Mk. 3 on the rain-soaked front straight.

Revson's McLaren M6B pulls away from Dan Gurney's McEagle during the early laps of the 1968 Bridgehampton Can-Am. Revson ran in the first five places prior to his departure from the race on the 48th lap due to a broken left rear suspension wishbone and upright.

When the 1968 Can-Am series moved north to Edmonton, Canada, Peter Revson qualified fifth overall. By the time the Shelby team finished racing at Edmonton they had determined that their McLaren could not run with Denis Hulme or Jim Hall but that the car was very competitive with the rest of the field, including Bruce McLaren's factory M8A.

In a close race for fourth place at Edmonton, Mark Donohue's (6) McLaren M6B leads Peter Revson's (52) McLaren M6B and Dan Gurney's (48) McEagle. On the 57th lap, Revson spun the rod bearing of his Ford engine and retired from the race.

Denis Hulme's (5) McLaren M8A leads a powerful field of cars toward the first corner at Stardust International Raceway. Bruce McLaren's (4) McLaren M8A, Jim Hall's (66) Chaparral 2G, Dan Gurney's (48) McEagle, Sam Posey's (1) Lola T160, and Peter Revson's (52) McLaren M6B follow close behind.

Mike Donovan (left) stands by as Carroll Smith (left) helps fuel the McLaren prior to the start of practice for the last Can-Am of the year, at Las Vegas. Revson qualified eighth for this race.

The first corner seems to be suffering from a traffic jam during the early laps of the Las Vegas race. Revson's (52) McLaren M6B leads Sam Posey's (1) Lola T160, Jerry Titus' (17) McLaren M6B, Chris Amon's (23) Ferrari 612, Charlie Hayes' (25) McKee Mk. 7, and Chuck Parsons' (10) Lola T160. Soon after this photo was taken, most of these cars would be taking evasive action to avoid a collision among the front runners.

After 55 laps at Las Vegas, Revson retired with suspension problems. After the 1968 Can-Am season was over, Revson ran the Shelby McLaren in a Can-Am-style race at Fuji Speedway in Japan and won that race by several laps. When the car returned to the United States, it was turned over to Holman & Moody, who ran it in 1969 with Mario Andretti as the driver. As for Shelby, his Can-Am career was over.

# 4 The Mustang GT 350

**It** was a project that, at first, no one at Shelby American wanted.

In mid-1964, Lee Iacocca told Ray Geddes, head of Ford's sports car division, to get the Mustang qualified for sports car racing and to get Carroll Shelby involved. Shelby, however, showed little interest when approached.

Looking back, one of the biggest reasons for Shelby's initial lack of interest could have been the shortage of space and manpower at our tiny Venice, California, shop. The Venice racing shop that we worked in between 1962 and 1965 was the old Reventlow shop, where Woolworth heir Lance Reventlow had built his Scarabs. Because Shelby took the shop over just after Reventlow left, we absorbed most of his equipment and some of his employees. The shop was adequate in the beginning, but as the company grew and the workload increased, it became overcrowded and difficult to work in. The shop bordered a residential area and I will never understand how the neighbors put up with the engine dyno running day and night and the continuous sound of racing cars being loaded and unloaded from our transporters, mostly in the late evening or after dark.

Shooting photographs in the race shop was no problem, because there was always room for me to

This is a well-known publicity photograph of the R Model Mustangs under construction at the Shelby Imperial plant in mid-1965. This is obviously a staged picture, but the shop was always spotless and the people, for the most part, were in clean whites. At least they were when they got to work. Even the shop that we had in Venice, although cluttered, was clean and orderly.

John Scott's (17) Shelby Mustang GT 350 leads Don Skogmo's (31) Genie Ford, Al Durham's (7) Ferrari GTB, and Peter Revson's (52) Brabham Climax during some of the close competition seen in the 1965 Nassau Trophy Race. Scott and Durham did not finish, Skogmo finished 31st, and Revson finished third overall.

This is one of the first Mustangs that was shipped by Ford to the Shelby American facility in Venice, California, during the summer of 1964. It is not known, or remembered, whether this car became the prototype street car or one of the first racing cars. The car pictured here was red in color, not white as many other sources report. Several white Mustangs were delivered at a later time.

work. Most of the race team personnel loved being photographed at work and most of them collected, and still have, the pictures that I took during that time. As the workload increased and space grew short, I relied more on wide-angle lenses and ladders to work from. Since the lighting in the shop was quite good, I shot most of my photographs with available light. I used a flash only as a last resort when there was no light available or to fill in shadow areas. (I have always felt that flash photography destroys the mood and can, in many cases, distract the subjects you are trying to capture on film. I find this particularly true today in my work with ballet companies. Flash was also a cardinal sin on the motion picture sets on which I worked for 25 years.)

By the middle of 1964, our tiny two-building company was bursting at the seams. The race shop was trying to contend with the building and upkeep of four King Cobras, two Ford GT40s, a Sunbeam Tiger, the lightweight 390-ci Cobra, the first 427-ci factory race car, six Daytona Coupes, and numerous factory and customer 289-ci Cobras.

The bottom line was that we were out of space and out of manpower. The ever-increasing popularity of the street version of the 289 Cobra had the production shop rushing about trying to keep pace with mounting orders. The production shop was also involved in a full-scale drag racing effort that took an additional toll on the time of the employees assigned to that department.

Finally, Geddes was able to convince Shelby that, if nothing else, the Mustang project was a good political move, and the first fastback Mustangs were shipped to the Venice shop in mid-1964. I photographed the first cars when they arrived, but since I was primarily involved with the racing program at that time, I only took a few photos of the prototype race car and the prototype street car. I remember taking several photos of the race car just before it went to Riverside or Willow Springs for a test session, and I worked with Pete Brock while he was creating the striping that would appear on the car once it went into production.

Like most of the people who worked at Shelby American at that time, I considered the Mustang program a waste of time, and I didn't give it much thought. Our primary focus had always been the Cobra and the Ford GT programs. That was what had put us on the map and kept us there. Those successful racing programs had delivered many customers to us and created a tremendous amount of publicity both for Shelby American and Ford Motor Company. I always felt, with some prejudice, that we should have devoted the lion's share of our time to the Cobra and GT projects. My reasoning was simple and a little selfish: Those projects had made the company in the first place, and they were the ones that I most enjoyed working on. Besides, I loved going racing, and the racing team was my main job.

Ford wanted to have these Mustangs ready to race for the beginning of the 1965 SCCA season. This created a very serious problem for Shelby, since the SCCA would not homologate the car unless 100 cars were completed by January 1, 1965. I wasn't there when the inspection occurred, but I can tell you that there was a major rush to complete the cars necessary. Somehow, as if by magic, when the SCCA inspectors appeared at Shelby American to authenticate that 100 cars had been built, there they were: 100 Mustang GT 350s all lined up for all to see. Thank goodness no one looked too closely because many of the Mustangs would not have passed a close inspection, especially if we had been required to start up each and every car. I think most of the production folks took the inspection fairly lightly because they knew that once Shelby got hold of the inspectors, things would be fine. A sham, of course, but it had to be done as the rules dictated.

By the time this inspection occurred, Shelby American had moved to the airport facility. Unlike the Venice shops, where everyone knew everyone and people would work in either the race or production shop, the two shops at the airport were almost completely separate. The company lost its character as it grew, and there wasn't the close camaraderie we had enjoyed in Venice. Few of us on the race side knew anyone in the production department or cared what transpired there.

By 1965, most of the better SCCA drivers had moved on to compete in the professional series that were coming into their own at that time, and the club racing arena of the SCCA lost much of the glamour and prestige that it had maintained in the fifties and early sixties.

The Mustang GT 350 raced mostly in this club racing environment, and it was in this venue that the Shelby-built Mustang succeeded beyond anyone's wildest dreams. Over the next three seasons, the Mustang GT 350 won numerous club events and three National B Production championships. Occasionally during this period, several of the GT 350s were run in the professional USRRC Manufacturer's

Championship races, but they were hopelessly out-classed by the Cobras, Ferrari GTOs, Porsche 904s, and Corvettes that they faced in this type of racing. Also, Mustang GT 350s were raced at Daytona, Sebring, and LeMans, but once again, they were completely outclassed by the competition they faced and they could only hope that their reliability could provide a good finishing position.

I'm sure from a business and a financial standpoint, the GT 350 was profitable, though as a purist, I will always feel that the GT 350 program was a distraction from our primary goal, racing. However, I can't deny that the program was lucrative, because it not only sold cars but generated a very large accessory market.

The photographs I am presenting in this chapter are not from the club events but from the professional and endurance events in which the Mustang GT 350 competed. There are two good reasons for this selection. For one thing, by the time the GT 350 started competing, I no longer had the time or the interest to photograph club events since, the Can-Am, Trans-Am, USRRC, and the World Manufacturer's Championship were where the action was. Second, almost no pictures of the Mustangs competing

This was the first prototype racing GT 350 that was completed at the Venice shop in early 1965. The car was basically used as a rolling test lab for future improvements and developments that would be incorporated into the future R Model Mustangs.

in the professional events have ever been published, and few people are even aware that the Mustangs competed in these events.

The Mustang GT 350 must be considered an important part of the legacy of Shelby American. Shelby gave the world a product that was a "race ready" car that anyone could buy from a Ford dealer, put on a trailer, and go racing. That in itself made the car unique and illustrated to the public that the common man, or woman, could go racing on a small budget, and, if one had some measure of talent, be reasonably successful. In today's racing climate things like that just aren't possible.

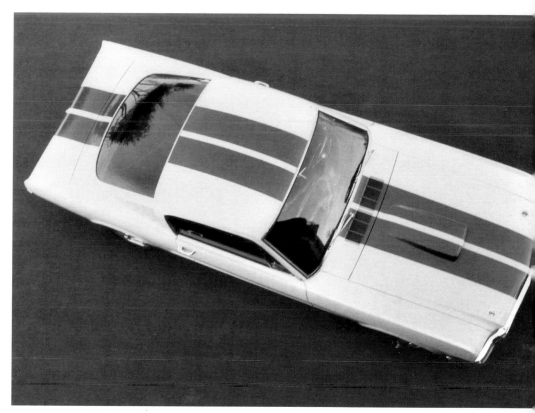

This was one of the very early production model GT 350 Mustangs that we used for some of the first advertising photos. These photos, taken from the top floor of an apartment complex in Marina Del Rey, illustrate the soon-to-become-famous striping that was designed by Pete Brock.

This Mustang GT 350 was one of the most photographed of all of the Shelby cars that appeared at a press preview prior to the running of the April 1965 USRRC race at Riverside.

This Dick Carter-driven, Hayward Ford-sponsored Mustang GT 350 was one of the earliest racing models, if not the earliest, seen in SCCA competition on the West Coast. Carter won the B Production race and finished ninth overall in the USRRC Manufacturer's Championship race at Laguna Seca in May 1965.

This is what the well-used Shelby Mustang looks like after the conclusion of a very rainy 200-mile race. Dick Jordan drove this entry to a 14th overall and 5th in the B Production class at the Badger 200. This race was run as a prelude to the Road America 500 in September 1965.

These two Comstock Racing Team Mustang GT 350s appeared at the Player's Quebec race at St. Jovite in September 1965. In the Sports Cars over 1,600-cc class (shown here), Eppie Wietzes (94) finished sixth overall while Walt MacKay (93) finished eighth overall. Although the Mustangs ran well, they were clearly outclassed by the Cobras, Porsches, and Corvettes that they opposed in this race.

This GT 350, raced by Scuderia Filipinetti, was one of the first Shelby Mustangs to be raced in Europe.

The Mustang of either Craig Fisher or Walt MacKay briefly leads the Ferrari 330 P2 (25) of David Piper and the Lotus 23 (101) of Bob McLean in Quebec. This Mustang did not finish, Piper finished second overall, and McLean was disqualified for a push start. It is interesting to note the very unusual hood scoop mounted on this Mustang. The reason for this modification to the hood scoop is unknown.

One of the things that drives any author trying to do proper research nuts is an "official" race record that shows a car being driven by two different drivers in the same race. Such a case is illustrated here, where either Craig Fisher or Walt MacKay (depending on which page of the official race results I look at) is driving the Mustang pictured here. Both of the Comstock Mustangs were also entered in the Player's Quebec feature race, and Eppie Wietzes finished 12th overall against some of the best modified sports cars in the world. Norm Evenden's (55) Cooper-Chevrolet and David Hobbs' (3) Lola T70 prepare to lap the Comstock Mustang. The Comstock Racing Team was the official Ford of Canada racing team and was very active at many of the North American venues for several years.

John Cordts' (104) Corvette brakes hard as he chases the Mustang of Eppie Weitzes during the production car race at Mosport. Cordts never passed Weitzes and finished fifth overall, while Weitzes finished third overall.

The two Comstock Racing Mustangs appeared at the Canadian Grand Prix for Sports Cars run at Mosport Park in September 1965. Eppie Weitzes (94) and Craig Fisher (93) finished third and fourth, respectively, behind the Cobras of Dan Gerber and Jean Ouellet in the production sports cars race, and they also ran in the featured race.

Both of the Comstock Mustangs came back to compete in the 1965 Canadian Grand Prix against an international field of top-notch modified sports cars. As was so often the case in the sixties, the field contained a combination of both GT and modified cars, and the GT cars had to carefully watch their rearview mirrors for the approach of the much faster sports cars. Eppie Weitzes (94) stays out of the way as Jim Hall's (66) Chaparral 2 and Jerry Hansen's (44) Chevette lap the slower Mustangs. Craig Fisher (93) trails the field.

Eppie Weitzes finished 14th overall and 14 laps behind Jim Hall and his Chaparral 2 in the 1965 Canadian Grand Prix.

Craig Fisher finished 15th overall in the 1965 Canadian Grand Prix.

As the green flag falls on the Nassau Tourist Trophy race in December 1965, Charlie Kolb's (7) Ferrari GTB, Tom Payne's (11) Shelby Cobra 289, Bob Grossman's (7) Ferrari GTO, Jack Ryan's (68) Porsche 904, Ben Warren, Jr.'s (17) Shelby Mustang GT 350, and Carmela Giuffre's (81) Abarth Simca charge down the front straight toward the first corner of the very rough Oakes Field circuit. Kolb was the winner and Warren did not finish.

Ben Warren's (17) Shelby Mustang GT 350 leads Ed Hamill's (60) Hamill Special, and R. Leitzinger's (99) Lotus Elan during the 1965 Nassau Governor's Trophy Race. Hamill finished third, Leitzinger finished 14th, and Warren did not finish.

The Mustang of Roger West and Richard Macon (99) leads the Donohue/Hansgen (95) Ford Mk. II and the MGB (44) of Ernie Croucher and Walter Glenn through the banking of the fourth turn during the 1966 Daytona 24 Hour race. The Donohue/Hansgen Ford Mk. II finished third overall while the Mustang and the MGB did not finish.

This Mustang driven by Don Kearney and Michael Reina finished 18th overall at Daytona in 1966 while the Dan Gerber/Bob Johnson/Hans Peter Lerch Shelby Cobra 289 (behind the Mustang) did not finish.

There were three GT 350s entered at Sebring in 1966, but only one started the race: one driven by Terry Kohler, Les Behm, and Walt Biddle. It went out of the race after just 71 laps with transmission trouble.

Engine failure and a broken left front wheel both contributed to a day when Eppie Wietzes shouldn't have gotten out of bed. These problems occurred during the June 1966 Production Car race at Mosport. Wietzes was to have driven this car in the Player's 200, but obviously he didn't make it.

David Ott's (1) Corvette, David Pabst's (17) Mustang GT 350, Terry Kohler's (82) Mustang GT 350, Randy Scheffer's (25) Corvette, Jim Spencer's (53) Yenko Stinger, and Frank Rieman's (16) Corvette prepare to start the September 1966 Badger 200 at Road America.

David Pabst finished third overall and second in B Production in the 1966 Badger 200.

Terry Kohler leads the 1966 Badger 200's eventual overall winner, David Ott. Ott was also the winner of the B Production class.

Terry Kohler finished fourth overall and third in B Production in the 1966 Badger 200.

Terry Kohler passes the Mustang GT 350 of Richard
Jordan in the 1966 Badger 200. Jordan did not
finish the race.

Anita Taylor drove this Mustang to 24th overall in the
1966 combined Governor's Trophy and Nassau
Tourist Trophy race. Taylor also drove this car in the
Nassau Trophy race, where she did not finish.

Some of the practice for the 1967 Sebring race was held in the rain. The Van Beuren/Jett Mustang ran well in the wet and qualified mid-field.

Four Mustang GT 350s participated in the 1967 Sebring race, and all are visible (if you really look) in this picture of the Le Mans start. The Fred Van Beuren/Paul Jett Mustang (18) gets a great start and is away with the early leaders.

As the late starters get away, three of the four Mustang GT 350s can be seen behind the Ford GTs of Bob Grossman/William McNamara (17) and Umberto Maglioli/Nino Vaccarella (19). Paul Richards (71) is the most prominent (just behind Grossman) with Bobby Allison (70) and Tom Yeager (16) farther back.

The GT 350 of Brad Booker/Tom Yeager doesn't seem to be paying any attention to the warning sign in the foreground. This car finished 28th overall at Sebring in 1967.

The Paul Richards Mustang overtakes the Porsche 911S of Andrea de Adamich and Teodoro Zeccoli early in the 1967 Sebring race. This Mustang retired from the race with a blown engine after just 22 laps.

The Mustang of Van Beuren/Jett finished 16th overall and was the highest-placed Mustang at Sebring in 1967. Although it placed well down in the GT category, the car won its particular GT class.

Well-known stock car driver Bobby Allison and Roger West drove this Mustang hard until it was involved in an accident on the 26th lap and did not finish the 1967 Sebring race.

The only Mustang GT 350 to ever race at Le Mans sits in the pits during practice surrounded by Fords and Ferraris. Unfortunately this Mustang appeared in 1967, where anything, no matter how notable, was overshadowed by the spectacular battle between Ford, Ferrari, Chaparral, Lola-Aston Martin, and Porsche. Claude Dubois and Chris Tuerlinx were the Mustang drivers.

After starting 52nd at Le Mans in 1967, Debois and Tuerlinx had worked their way up to 41st place by the seventh hour. It was at this point that the gearbox failed and put them out of the competition.

The biggest problems at Le Mans for a car like the Mustang was to keep out of the way of the big boys, who were probably 50 to 80 miles per hour faster on the long Mulsanne straight.

The Trans-Am Series began in 1966 as a racing series for the small sedans or "pony cars" that were being produced by the Detroit auto makers at that time. These cars—Mustangs, Camaros, Cougars, Barracudas, Matadors, Challengers, and Firebirds—were very popular with America's youth. Between 1967 and 1970, the series developed into a hugely popular, slam-bang racing series that was contested at one time or another by most of the top racing drivers and manufacturers in America. All of these races took place on the top roadracing circuits across the country, and close, fender-banging races became the rule, not the exception.

When the series opened with its first race at Sebring in March 1966, Shelby American was totally committed to the Ford GT program and had no interest in the Trans-Am series. As the season progressed, however, Ford prevailed upon Shelby to prepare a number of customer cars. When, near the end

Jerry Titus and his Shelby Mustang prepare to qualify for the first Trans-Am race of 1967. The race, held one day prior to the Daytona Continental 24 Hour race, featured all of the future stars of the series and was a preview of the close, metal-bending action that would excite fans from coast to coast over the next four seasons. For the 1967 season, Shelby American, under the direction of Project Engineer Chuck Cantwell, built four team cars for team drivers Dick Thompson and Jerry Titus. Shelby also built 22 additional Trans-Am Mustangs for independent racers to use in the Trans-Am or SCCA A Sedan racing. This was an era in which independent drivers and teams could be competitive and, under the right circumstances, even win a professional event. Shelby didn't hesitate to supply race-ready Mustangs at friendly prices to those who wanted to be weekend racers in a reasonably competitive car.

Peter Revson was the only Shelby entry at Watkins Glen in 1969. Since there were only four days to rebuild the wrecked cars after the Quebec race, the Shelby team was the odd man out when only three Mustangs could be prepared by Kar Kraft.

The first Trans-Am race, a four-hour event, was held in conjunction with the 1966 Sebring race. Although Shelby did not build any Mustangs for this race, his eye was on the possibilities created by this new professional race series. Later in the season, Shelby American would build several Mustangs for the series and would also supply parts to the other Ford competitors. A. J. Foyt's Mustang (4) leads the field away from the start of that first race.

of the season, Ford had a chance to win the championship, the company called upon Shelby to build a team car for the final race of the year. When the series reached Riverside for the last race, Ford and Chrysler were tied for the points lead with 37 points each, and it became Shelby's assignment to win the championship. It turned out to be a storybook finish. Jerry Titus suffered a bad start when he flooded his engine during the Le Mans start, but he overcame it and moved up from 31st place to take the lead on the 95th lap, ultimately winning the race and the championship for Ford.

Shelby's reward for his work in 1966 was a budget to field a full factory team effort for 1967. One must remember that during the Trans-Am glory years (1966–1970) only the manufacturers got championship points and, consequently, most of the glory and publicity. There was no driver's championship during that time, and for that reason drivers really didn't get their just rewards. Titus' reward for his deeds in 1966 was a factory ride in 1967.

If 1966 was a trial year, then 1967 was the year that the Trans-Am came into full bloom. Shelby American had helped Ford win the title the previous

year and the company was rewarded with the opportunity to field a full factory-backed team for the 12-race 1967 season. Jerry Titus would be the team leader and he would be backed up by Dr. Dick Thompson (until Thompson retired from racing in the middle of the season). Milt Minter, Jim Adams, and Ronnie Bucknum shared the second car after Thompson's retirement. Ford had also invested a great deal of money in the Mercury Cougar effort that was run by well-known stock car team owner Bud Moore.

Titus had a great season for the Shelby team and won four races. But by the season finale at Kent, Washington, the Mustang team was trailing the Cougar team by a single point. Once again, it came down to the final race to determine the championship, and the best writers in Hollywood couldn't have scripted a better storybook ending. The complete story is told via photos and captions later in the chapter, but basically, Ronnie Bucknum won the championship for Mustang, finishing second, ahead of Dan Gurney's third-place Cougar.

For the Shelby Mustang team, coming off two consecutive championships, 1968 looked like it could be another banner year. It started well, too, as Titus

Dr. Dick Thompson drove a Mustang in that first Trans-Am race. Thompson would become a Shelby team driver in 1967. Little is known or remembered about that first race at Sebring. No one cared about the new, upstart series at that time and there was almost no press coverage given to the race. This would change drastically by 1967.

The legendary A. J. Foyt (shown here) drove his only Trans-Am race at Sebring. Foyt led the first 13 laps but went out of the race with engine problems. The race was won by none other then future world champion Jochen Rindt, driving an under-2-liter Alfa Romeo GTA.

and Bucknum shared the class victory and a fourth overall at the 24 Hours of Daytona. This was the first race of the season and it was a great way to start. But after Daytona, it was downhill all the way, due to continued Ford engine disasters. Titus and Horst Kwech, who joined the team as the number two driver, found their efforts hampered all season by Ford-induced engine problems. The team was only able to win three of the 13 races. Frustration over the engine problems and Ford's attitude caused a season of dissension among the team members, and caused Titus' departure before the season's end.

The engine used by the Shelby team in the Trans-Am series in 1967 was the tried-and-true 289-cubic-inch Ford engine with a slight overbore. The team knew this engine well, because it had been used in most of the race victories that Shelby American had achieved since the company was begun in 1962. Noticeable modifications are the aluminum intake manifold, twin four-barrel Holly carburetors, and the drag racing-style headers.

Jerry Titus qualified third fastest in 1967 behind the Bud Moore Mercury Cougars of Parnelli Jones and Dan Gurney. It is important to remember that although the names of Titus, Mark Donohue, and Parnelli Jones are synonymous with the Trans-Am championships from 1967 to 1971, there was no official driver's championship in the series until 1972. All championship points awarded, during what is remembered as the Golden Era (1967–1971) of the series were given to the manufacturer, not the driver. This was what kept the manufacturer participation at such a high level during this period. Once the Driver's Championship was instituted, the manufacturer's participation disappeared.

Dr. Dick Thompson (12), the well-known racing dentist from Washington, D.C., leads Dan Gurney's (16) Mercury Cougar through the infield at Daytona in 1967. Thompson, sponsored by Gulf Oil, was Shelby's second team driver until he decided to retire at mid-season. All of the 26 Shelby Mustangs that were built for the 1967 season were available in one color: white. Thompson led the Daytona race until his clutch blew.

Jerry Titus' (68) Mustang and Parnelli Jones' (16) Mercury Cougar stage a furious battle for the lead. Both of these drivers led at one point or another during the race, but Parnelli fell back with engine problems while Titus blew a tire after colliding with Bill Bowman's Porsche on the high banks and finished fourth overall.

The problems suffered by the Trans-Am team were also felt in the shop at home. By 1968, Shelby American had closed the airport facility and moved its operation to a small shop in Torrance, California. Operating as Shelby Racing Company, this shop had only enough room to store and maintain the Trans-Am and Can-Am cars. Only a few of the long-time racing employees were retained after this move.

Nineteen sixty-eight was a contentious season for the Shelby team. Most of the in-fighting was created by the lack of support from Ford and its pitiful engine preparation. Naturally, the drivers blamed the problems on the mechanics, since they prepared the cars and were the first ones seen in the pits by the drivers after an engine blowup. The mechanics, in turn, blamed Ford but none of the Engine and Foundry people were ever at the races to witness the problems first hand.

In 1969, Ford introduced the new Boss 302 Mustang into Trans-Am competition, and the regular Shelby team drivers—Peter Revson, Horst Kwech and, occasionally, Dan Gurney—looked forward to a more enjoyable season. Unfortunately for the Shelby effort, though, Ford brought the Bud Moore team back into Trans-Am racing after a year's absence, and the majority of Ford's money and effort seemed to go

to Moore's team. Once again, nothing seemed to go right for the Shelby team and on more than one occasion, tempers flared between the drivers and crew members.

The only win during the 1969 season came at Lime Rock with Sam Posey winning as he filled in for Revson, who was busy qualifying at Indianapolis. Several third-place finishes filled out what was a very disappointing year.

After Riverside, the last event of the 1969 season, it was decided that the Shelby racing effort would be terminated. For Shelby American, it was a good time to quit, as there was nothing further to win. Shelby himself had grown tired of the political battles, and his interest in racing wasn't what it had been in the beginning. Shelby American had done its thing, and the company had achieved far more than anyone could have ever imagined. We created a legend in our own lifetime and not too many people can claim they were part of such an undertaking. The legend we created 30 years ago is bigger today than ever. At the time, we all just thought we were doing our jobs. No one had any idea that what we were doing would be remembered at all, let alone decades later.

We were a pretty cocky lot back then, and I guess we had good reason to be!

The two names that dominated the Trans-Am scene during the early years were Jerry Titus and Mark Donohue, and here they show why. Close, no-quarter-given racing was what the early Trans-Am was all about, and these two drivers were always right in the thick of the action. Daytona was the first race for the Penske Sunoco Z28 Camaro, and although the car suffered from handling, brake, and engine problems, Donohue proved that the car had serious potential.

Dick Thompson leads the Plymouth Barracuda (22) of Frank Karmatz out of the infield onto Daytona's famed banked oval. Notice how clean these cars looked before runaway commercialism took over.

Titus' Mustang is prepared for the 1967 Four Hour Trans-Am Race that was run the day before the famous Sebring 12-hour race. Team engineer Chuck Cantwell can be seen at the far left while team manager Lew Spencer can be seen at the far right in the checkered shirt. Note the "Team Terilingua" emblazoned on the car. Terlingua was a small Texas town were Shelby held his first chili cookoff.

Dick Thompson's Mustang is pushed into third starting position under the watchful eye of Carroll Shelby.

Jerry Titus (17) won the 1967 Sebring pole position from Parnelli Jones (15) with a time of 3:10.0 around the rough Sebring course. Third-fastest was Dick Thompson (11), followed by Mark Donohue (6) and Dan Gurney (16). The Sebring race was run on an old, deserted air base. The track was very rough in places, but it was a safe place to race for the most part because there was so much run-off room. Because the track was marked by cones—which were usually knocked down by the end of the first hour—many of the drivers got lost in the dark or in bad weather and there were some interesting off-course excursions. For the era, the pits and track accommodations were quite adequate for the drivers and crews.

Dick Thompson finished third overall in the four-hour race at Sebring in 1967.

Jerry Titus won his first 1967 Trans-Am race at Sebring, beating Mark Donohue's much-improved Camaro.

Dick Thompson (11) and Mark Donohue (6) battle for second position. By the end of the four-hour race, the positions were reversed. Note the dragging tailpipe on Thompson's car.

Jerry Titus and Carroll Shelby formed a dynamic team during the early years of the Trans-Am. Titus' aggressive style was made for Trans-Am racing. His mechanical experience served the Shelby team well, because he knew how to relate any car problems he was having to the mechanics in a language they could understand. If there was any knock on Titus' ability, it was that he was a crasher and very hard on his car.

Dick Thompson, Jerry Titus, and Ronnie Bucknum were the key drivers for the Shelby Mustang team in 1967.

When the Trans-Am season moved to Green Valley, Texas, in April 1967, Jerry Titus started off the action by rolling his Mustang in practice.

Is this what a "Shelby Race Prepared" Mustang is supposed to look like?

Dick Thompson started on the pole position with a time of 1:14.4, which happened to be the same that Dan Gurney (98) posted for second position.

Jerry Titus started the 1967 Green Valley race in last (30th) position. His badly damaged car had been repaired overnight although it was strongly rumored that Shelby had replaced it with a spare.

By the time the 1967 Texas race was 30 laps old, Titus had taken the lead. Here he leads his teammate Dick Thompson (11), Milt Minter's (78) Mustang, John McComb's (33) Mustang, and Parnelli Jones' (15) Mercury Cougar.

Dick Thompson demonstrates the latest in prototype air brakes at Lime Rock in 1967. After this accident on the first lap, Thompson slowly made his way back to the pits for repairs. Unfortunately the repairs were to no avail because the car broke before the end of the race.

The 1967 Green Valley Trans-Am was run on an extremely hot and humid day and the race took its toll on Jerry Titus' chances for victory. On lap 114, Titus, suffering from extreme heat exhaustion, had to be replaced by Ron Dykes. The Titus/Dykes Mustang finished fifth overall.

Because of previous racing commitments, several of the Trans-Am regulars were not available when the series moved to Mid Ohio in June 1967. NASCAR champion David Pearson, subbing for Dan Gurney, qualified for the pole position and took the lead when the green flag fell. Pearson led the first lap and then Jerry Titus (17) took over and led the next 125 laps to the checkered flag. Following Titus is Ed Leslie in a Mercury Cougar, Fred Van Beuren's Mustang, and Jim Adams, subbing for Dick Thompson, in the Gulf Oil Mustang.

Jim Adams had his first Trans-Am ride in the Shelby/Gulf Oil Mustang at Mid Ohio in June 1967.

Jerry Titus laps Horst Kwech's (8) Alfa Romeo at Mid Ohio in June 1967. Titus won the race overall, and Kwech won the under-2-liter category and finished fourth overall.

Jim Adams makes an unexpected pit stop because of an engine fire at Mid Ohio in June 1967. Adams did not continue.

Jerry Titus makes a routine pit stop at Mid Ohio. There were no limits on how many people could be over the pit wall during a Trans-Am pit stop. The pit stops were well choreographed and the factory-backed teams had fast, efficient stops. One can't compare the pit stops of that era with the pit stops of today because of the great advances in pit equipment technology.

At Mid Ohio, Jerry Titus became the first driver to win two Trans-Am races during the 1967 season.

There's a serious discussion going on in the garage area of Riverside Raceway. Team manager Lew Spencer (center) is deep in thought, as are Ronnie Bucknum (left) and Jerry Titus (right). Lew Spencer was a popular, top-rated West Coast production driver during the late fifties and early sixties. He signed on with Shelby American in March 1963, driving his first race in a Cobra at Sebring the same year. Spencer contributed to many of the long distance race victories that the Shelby team achieved between 1963 and 1965. Spencer became the Trans-Am team manager in 1967 and retained that job until the team left racing at the end of the 1969 season. Because he had been a driver and a dealership owner, Spencer could deal with the drivers and the mechanics on an equal footing. Ronnie Bucknum was one of the top production car drivers in the country when Honda picked him to become its first Formula One driver in 1964. Bucknum drove for several of the top Trans-Am teams, and he was a driver that could always be counted on in the clutch.

Jerry Titus seems pleased with winning the pole position for the 1967 Mission Bell 250, which is what they called the Riverside Trans-Am race.

Jerry Titus (17) won his fourth Trans-Am race of 1967 at Crow's Landing in northern California. Following Titus is Milt Minter's (78) Mustang, which finished fourth overall. Peter Revson (behind Minter) finished second overall in a Mercury Cougar.

Spectators watch the preparation of the Shelby team Mustangs at Riverside prior to the 1967 Trans Am race.

David Pearson's Cougar (15) drafts Jerry Titus' (17) Mustang into the Riverside esses. The two cars raced like this for the first 16 laps until Titus pitted with a bad front end vibration, giving the lead, and the win, to Pearson.

Team mechanic Bobby Boxx (right) and a helper prepare to re-install the transmission in one of the Shelby Mustangs.

When the 1967 Trans-Am series moved to Kent, Washington, for the season's final Mercury led Ford by one point (60 to 59) in the Manufacturer's Championship. Obviously the race at Kent was an all-or-nothing event for both marques. The Shelby Mustang effort suffered a serious setback when Jerry Titus destroyed his car during a Saturday qualifying session. The Bud Moore crew in the background analyzes their newfound luck.

Dan Gurney, early in the 1963 Sebring race. Soon this car would begin suffering from many of the numerous problems that plagued the Shelby team that day. This car was the only factory Cobra that finished (23rd place) the race.

Dave MacDonald at Sebring in 1963.

Ken Miles loses a wheel during the 1964 *L.A. Times* Grand Prix at Riverside.

Dan Gerber, one of the best-known of the independent Cobra drivers, had the usual bad Cobra luck at Nassau in 1964 and did not finish any of the races that he entered.

Tom Payne finished fifth overall in the 1964 Nassau Tourist Trophy race and ninth in the Governor's Trophy race. Payne failed to finish the Nassau Trophy race.

Ken Miles debuted the 390 Cobra in a spectacular, if only brief, manner during the 1964 Nassau Trophy race. Miles led briefly before blowing the engine.

Ken Miles tried his luck once again in 1964 in the Nassau Trophy race but, once again, was forced out with a blown engine. These and several other color shots that I took at Nassau may be the only color action pictures that exist of this car.

This is the only known color photograph of Chris Amon testing the first 427 Cobra that was built at AC Cars in the fall of 1964. This test took place at Silverstone. Note the large bulge in the hood.

This Ford GT40 was the first of its breed to finish and win a race. Ken Miles and Lloyd Ruby won the 1965 Daytona Continental in this car.

Bob Bondurant and Richie Ginther finished third overall at Daytona in 1965 in this GT40.

Ronnie Bucknum drove a very consistent race to finish sixth overall in the 1964 Monterey Grand Prix run at Laguna Seca.

Dave MacDonald heads for Riverside's Turn 1 during the 1963 *L.A. Times* Grand Prix. In defeating a large international field of cars and drivers, the relatively unknown MacDonald served notice that with the right equipment he would be a major player in the future.

By late in the 1963 *L.A. Times* race MacDonald had lapped the entire field. This was something that no one else had ever done, due to the strong competition that this race attracted. As MacDonald heads through Turn 7, his only thoughts were on finishing the race without any major problem.

Lew Spencer and his crew, Ted Sutton (left) and Jim O'Leary (right), pose for the camera just before going to Willow Springs in May 1964.

Jerry Titus (17) laps the Mustang of Mike Allison (22) early in the 1967 Green Valley Trans-Am. Titus had to be relieved by Ron Dykes due to heat stroke, and the car finished fifth overall. Allison did not finish.

Jerry Titus leads a Porsche 911 during the Lime Rock Trans-Am. Titus finished third in this race.

149

Ed Leslie's (97) Lang-Cooper leads Roger Penske's (66) Chaparral 2, Tommy Hitchcock's (21) Brabham BT8, Don Wester's (60) Genie-Ford, and Bill Krause's (28) Lotus 30 through Laguna Seca's Turn 1. Leslie went on to finish fifth overall and Penske took the overall win.

Bob Holbert's King Cobra enters Turn 7 during the 1963 *L.A. Times* Grand Prix Holbert was always one of the fastest drivers on the track, but he was continually hampered by overheating problems that, for some reason, seemed impossible to cure in his car.

At the 1968 Can-Am race in Edmonton, Alberta, Canada, Peter Revson qualified fifth overall. The Shelby team realized after this race that their McLaren could outrun most of the field, but probably not front-runners Denis Hulme and Jim Hall.

Ed Leslie drove his brightly painted Lang-Cooper to fifth overall at the 1964 Pacific Grand Prix.

Horst Kwech (2) provided a rare victory for the Shelby team at Riverside. Following Kwech is Browne Goodwin's Lancia Fulvia.

Peter Revson's Shelby Mustang at the 1969 Michigan International Speedway Trans-Am race. Revson did not finish.

Ronnie Bucknum confers with Jerry Titus (in car) during a pit stop at Sebring in 1968. Note the mechanic enlarging the wheelwell. Bucknum and Titus finished fifth overall and third in Trans-Am.

Ronnie Bucknum drove this Shelby Mustang to a second-place finish at the 1967 Stardust 350 staged in Las Vegas. Parnelli Jones (15) trails in his Bud Moore Mercury Cougar.

The Titus/Bucknum Shelby Mustang (1) laps the Boyce/Yuma Camaro and the Moore/Murphy Camaro during the 1968 Daytona 24 Hour race. The Shelby Mustang finished fourth overall and won the Trans-Am class.

Jerry Titus (17) and David Pearson (15) are racing for the lead as they enter Riverside's Turn 6. Pearson won the race and Titus went out with a serious vibration problem.

Ronnie Bucknum (left) watches as his crew changes tires and makes suspension adjustments under the car.

A bruised and battered Jerry Titus (left), Ronnie Bucknum (right), and independent Shelby Mustang driver Milt Minter (not pictured) were the standard-bearers for the Ford Mustang effort to clinch the 1967 Trans-Am championship. These three faced formidable competition with Dan Gurney, Parnelli Jones, and Alan Moffat driving the Bud Moore Mercury Cougars. Bucknum qualified his Mustang in fourth position behind Donohue, Jones, and Gurney.

After destroying his Mustang in qualifying at Kent, Titus took over John McComb's Shelby-built Mustang and qualified seventh on the grid.

Jerry Titus gives the lapped Camaro of Dave Phelan a slight wake-up call as he attempts to move up on the leaders at Kent in 1967. Titus retired on lap 65 with a blown engine, and privateer Milt Minter only lasted 11 laps before retiring with no oil pressure. At this point, it didn't look very good for the Mustang team.

Mark Donohue's (6) Sunoco Camaro, Ronnie Bucknum's (31) Shelby Mustang, and Parnelli Jones' (15) Mercury Cougar battle for the lead at Kent. The Cougar's hope for victory went up in smoke when Parnelli's car refused to start after a routine pit stop, and Dan Gurney was slowed by a flat tire, a broken windshield, and a leaking fuel cap.

Ronnie Bucknum (31) and Mark Donohue (6) race for the lead of the 1967 Kent race. Donohue won the race when Bucknum was slowed because of engine overheating.

The last half of the race was for second place and the 1967 Manufacturer's Championship. Ronnie Bucknum won the race of the walking wounded when he beat Dan Gurney's Cougar by 40 seconds for second place. The Ford Mustang had won its second-consecutive Trans-Am championship by just two points (64 to 62).

This was the team that won the 1967 Trans-Am Manufacturer's Championship for the Ford Mustang. Jerry Titus (left), Dick Thompson (center), and Ronnie Bucknum (right) surround a happy Carroll Shelby, who sits on a stack of (Goodyear, obviously) tires. Unfortunately for Titus, there was no official driver's championship in 1967, or any year until 1972.

In 1968, the Shelby Mustangs were driven by Jerry Titus (1) and Horst Kwech (2). Since the Trans-Am cars were now allowed to run in the 24 Hours of Daytona, Ronnie Bucknum was brought in to co-drive with Titus and Allan Moffat was brought in to co-drive with Kwech. Ford thought that its new 302-cubic-inch engine with high-performance tunnel-port heads was the hot setup for 1968, but was terribly wrong. What started off as a great year turned into disaster and chaos. The tunnel-port head was specially designed with wide mouth ports to increase air intake. The push rod tubes went through the intake ports rather than around them. This supposedly permitted bigger tunnel size, more air intake, and 15 percent more power. Unfortunately, when the engines ran on tracks with a lot of curves, the heads trapped oil and the engines blew.

Once again, the very capable Lew Spencer was the team manager for the Shelby effort in 1968.

Jerry Titus makes a routine pit stop and turns the Shelby Mustang over to Ronnie Bucknum at Daytona in 1968. This pair of drivers not only won the Trans-Am category but also finished an astonishing fourth overall against international competition.

The start of the Sebring 12 Hour race shows the incredible contrast in the types of machinery that showed up in 1968. If you look closely, you can see the Kwech/Moffat Shelby Mustang (32) up among the leading Porsches, Lolas, and Ford GT40s. Other Trans-Am cars that are visible are the Donohue/Fisher (15) Camaro, Titus/Bucknum (31) Shelby Mustang, Grant/Scott (25) AMC Javelin, and the Chitwood/Hoffman (17) Camaro. The Donohue/Fisher Camaro finished third overall and first in the Trans-Am class, while Titus/Bucknum finished fifth overall and third in Trans-Am. The Kwech/Moffat Shelby Mustang was withdrawn from the race after 3 hours and 40 minutes (63 laps) due to undisclosed problems. Could it have been the first of many engine failures that was to haunt Shelby's team for the rest of the season?

This pit board tells what each crew member's assignment is.

The Kwech/Moffat Mustang races through the night at Daytona in 1968. This car retired with suspension failure after 176 laps.

Parnelli Jones drove one of the Shelby Mustangs at the 1968 War Bonnet 250 in Tulsa, Oklahoma, and finished third overall, while Jerry Titus suffered from one of the team's many engine blowups and did not finish. Mark Donohue won the race in his Sunoco Camaro.

NASCAR champion David Pearson also drove one of the Shelby Mustangs in 1968. Pearson drove the car at Lime Rock and was the first car to retire (with a blown engine) from the race after only completing 22 laps. Jerry Titus finished second overall, two laps behind race winner Mark Donohue.

Dan Gurney drove two Trans-Am races (Watkins Glen 500 and the Continental Divide 250) for the Shelby Mustang team in 1968. Gurney blew engines in both of the races. The most frustrating problem with the tunnel-port engines was that the Shelby crew members, who had years of experience with 289-cubic-inch engines, were not allowed to touch or work on the Ford engines that were delivered to the shop.

Jerry Titus (1) leads the field away during the parade lap for the 1968 Mission Bell 250 Riverside Trans-Am race. This was to be Jerry's last race for the Shelby Mustang team. His frustration with the repeated engine problems— and Ford's failure to deal with them—had reached the breaking point, and Titus departed to race for Terry Godsall's Pontiac team. Behind Titus is eventual race winner Horst Kwech's (2) Shelby Mustang, George Follmer's (4) AMC Javelin, Peter Revson's (3) AMC Javelin, and Dick Guldstrand's (17) Camaro.

Enough said.

Mark Donohue's (6) Sunoco Camaro and Jerry Titus' (7) Shelby Mustang wage a furious battle for the lead during the early laps of the 1968 Riverside race. While in the lead on lap 15, Titus blew his engine again, leaving Donohue in the lead.

Praying that the engine will stay together at Riverside in 1968, Kwech leads the Javelins of Follmer (4) and Revson (3) late in the race.

Kwech pits for gas at Riverside in 1968. Note the dented fenders that were commonplace among Trans-Am competitors. Note the fuel pouring off the car's tail; refueling was very primitive by today's standards.

This sign says it all. Of the 13 Trans-Am races run in 1968, the Shelby Mustang won only three, while the Penske Sunoco Camaro won ten. This had not been a very even battlefield.

Horst Kwech receives his trophy from a charming American Airlines stewardess. After helping Ford win the 1966 and 1967 Trans-Am Manufacturer's Championship, the frustrations of the 1968 season had not done very much to enhance either Shelby's or Ford's racing reputation.

The ecstatic Shelby crew crowds around the winning car.

The 1969 Trans-Am season opened at Michigan International Raceway in May. The Shelby team had Peter Revson and Horst Kwech as drivers and the new fastback Boss 302 Mustangs with conventional 302-cubic-inch, 470 (rumored) brake horsepower engines. This horsepower gave the Ford teams of Shelby and Bud Moore a significant power advantage, but was that enough to beat the Penske Camaros? Horst Kwech (seen driving here) did not finish the race due to a serious accident caused by the less-than-desirable weather conditions.

This is the engine that powered the Boss 302 Mustangs in the 1969 Trans-Am. After the disastrous 1968 tunnel-port experiment, logical minds prevailed over corporate policy and the 1969 version of the 302-cubic-inch engine returned to conventional heads and more reliable horsepower.

The spartan but efficient cockpit of the 1969 Boss 302 Mustang. The water jug behind the seat provided drinking water for the driver during the race. A tube went from the jug to where the driver could easily access it during the race. We often toyed with the idea of pouring a bottle of 151-proof rum in that jug to see what might happen.

Next pages: Michigan was a team manager's nightmare. Talk about a tire dilemma? On race day, it rained, snowed, hailed, and was sunny. What's your tire choice?

Peter Revson qualified eighth at Michigan in 1969 and moved up quickly to take the lead on lap 17. By lap 21, however, Revson's engine was smoking heavily and he retired from the race with a blown engine.

Peter Revson, deep in thought.

The two Shelby Mustangs take their grid positions prior to the start of the 1969 St. Jovite Trans-Am. Peter Revson (1) qualified fourth while Horst Kwech (2) qualified eighth. Mark Donohue (6) qualified second.

Peter Revson on the move, but not for long. On the 15th lap, Revson was involved in an eight-car pileup that eliminated the entire Ford Mustang team and several others from the 1969 Quebec race.

Horst Kwech was also involved in the eight-car crash at Quebec. It always seemed that Kwech was in the wrong place at the wrong time, and although it was not always his fault, he wrecked three cars in seven races. After the disaster at St. Jovite, it was decided to replace Kwech with Dan Gurney, but Kwech returned to the team for the final two races at Kent and Riverside.

Parnelli Jones' (15) Bud Moore Mustang leads Peter Revson's (1) Shelby Mustang, Ron Grable's (3) AMC Javelin, Horst Kwech's (2) Shelby Mustang, Jerry Titus' (13) Pontiac Firebird, and the rest of the field through Turn 1. Titus had a better season in his Pontiac than did any of the Shelby drivers in their Mustangs. Titus finished third in the unofficial driver standings, while Shelby driver Peter Revson finished fourth. Considering Shelby's season-long performance, I'm sure Titus had no regrets about the move that he made.

Peter Revson enjoys a light moment during a break in the action at Watkins Glen in 1969.

The destruction of Kwech's car (shown here), along with Revson's car doomed the Shelby Trans-Am effort for the rest of the 1969 season. No matter what, or how much, the crew did, the cars would never work right again.

Peter Revson leads the Javelin of Ron Hunter at Watkins Glen in 1969.

Peter Revson is chased up the hill by Ed Leslie's (9) Sunoco Camaro and Rusty Jowett's (92) Camaro. On lap 76, Revson was bumped off the track by Leslie's Camaro and was unable to continue do to his off-course excursion.

This type of racing is what made the "Golden Years of the Trans-Am" so memorable. Peter Revson (1) and Parnelli Jones (15) battle for position during the 1969 Laguna Seca Trans-Am.

Peter Revson and Lew Spencer share a thought after Revson qualified in fourth position for the 1969 Watkins Glen Trans-Am.

As Dan Gurney (2) exits Turn 9 at Laguna Seca in 1969, Revson gets sideways in front of several lapped cars. John Hall (82) is in the Mustang at the end of the pack.

Dan Gurney stepped into Horst Kwech's car at Laguna Seca in 1969 and qualified eighth. Gurney could never get the car to handle to his liking, yet wound up finishing third overall.

Peter Revson leads lapped traffic through the fastest part of the beautiful Laguna Seca circuit in 1969. Parnelli Jones and George Follmer (at the end of the pack) prepare to lap the two back markers.

Revson leads Gerry Gregory (56) Camaro down the famous Laguna Seca corkscrew in 1969. Revson finished fourth overall behind Mark Donohue, Ed Leslie, and Dan Gurney.

For a brief moment at Kent in 1969, the two Shelby team Mustangs ran together. Peter Revson had qualified sixth overall, while Gurney qualified seventh overall.

Who do you think this young lady favored?

Dan Gurney laps Thomas Lynch's (74) Camaro on his way to a third place overall at Laguna Seca.

Carroll Shelby (left) always had a sympathetic ear, especially when it came to beautiful young ladies.

Dan Gurney leads eventual race winner Ronnie Bucknum's (9) Sunoco Camaro and Peter Gregg's (59) Porsche 911 at Kent in 1969. Gregg won the under-2-liter category.

The Shelby crew replaces Dan Gurney's broken windshield in record time at the 1969 Washington race. Flying rocks were always a hazard at Kent, and this was the second time that a broken windshield affected Gurney's performance in a three-year period. He had previously broken one while driving a Cougar for Bud Moore.

Peter Revson and Ronnie Bucknum race for position at Kent in 1969. Revson finished fourth overall behind Ronnie Bucknum, Parnelli Jones, and Jerry Titus.

The well-drilled Shelby crew gives Peter Revson maximum service in a minimum amount of time.

A sharply focused Peter Revson at speed.

At Riverside in 1969, Revson qualified fourth and finished fourth overall. This was the final race for the Shelby Mustangs and for the Shelby Racing Co. After eight glorious seasons, it had all come to an end.

# Appendix

## Shelby American Professional and FIA Race Record, 1962–1967

| No. | Driver | Car | Finish | Notes |
|-----|--------|-----|--------|-------|
| **RIVERSIDE 3-HOUR ENDURO RACE, OCTOBER 13, 1962** | | | | |
| 98 | Bill Krause | Shelby Cobra | DNF | First Race for the Cobra |
| **NASSAU TOURIST TROPHY, DECEMBER 2, 1962** | | | | |
| 98 | Bill Krause | Shelby Cobra | 26th Place | |
| 18 | Augie Pabst | Shelby Cobra | DNF | |
| 106 | John Everly | Shelby Cobra | DNF | |
| **NASSAU GOVERNOR'S TROPHY RACE, DECEMBER 7, 1962** | | | | |
| 98 | Bill Krause | Shelby Cobra | DNF | |
| 18 | Augie Pabst | Shelby Cobra | DNF | |
| **NASSAU TROPHY RACE, DECEMBER 9, 1962** | | | | |
| 106 | John Everly | Shelby Cobra | 26th overall | |
| **PACIFIC COAST CHAMPIONSHIP—RIVERSIDE, FEBRUARY 2 and 3, 1963** | | | | |
| 198 | Dave MacDonald | Shelby Cobra | 1st Place | First Cobra Win |
| 98 | Ken Miles | Shelby Cobra | 2nd Place | |
| **DAYTONA CONTINENTAL 3-HOUR RACE, FEBRUARY 17, 1963** | | | | |
| 99 | Dave MacDonald | Shelby Cobra | 4th overall | |
| 97 | Skip Hudson | Shelby Cobra | DNF | |
| 98 | Dan Gurney | Shelby Cobra | DNF | |
| **SEBRING 12-HOUR RACE, MARCH 23, 1963** | | | | |
| 12 | Phil Hill/Ken Miles/Ken Miles | Shelby Cobra | 11th overall | |
| 15 | Dan Gurney/Phil Hill | Shelby Cobra | 29th overall | |
| 11 | Jacko Maggiacomo/Peter Jopp | Shelby Cobra | 41st overall | |
| 16 | Ken Miles/Lew Spencer | Shelby Cobra | DNF | |
| 14 | Dave MacDonald/Glenn "Fireball" Roberts | Shelby Cobra | DNF | |
| **PENSACOLA USRRC MANUFACTURER'S RACE, MAY 26, 1963** | | | | |
| 45 | R. E. L. Hayes | Shelby Cobra | 5th overall | |
| 33 | Bob Johnson | Shelby Cobra | DNF | |
| 96 | Bob Holbert | Shelby Cobra | DNF | |
| 97 | Dave MacDonald | Shelby Cobra | DNF | |
| 98 | Ken Miles | Shelby Cobra | DNF | |
| **PLAYER'S 200–MOSPORT, CANADA, JUNE 1, 1963** | | | | |
| 54 | Eppie Wietzes | Shelby Cobra | 9th overall | |
| 33 | Bob Johnson | Shelby Cobra | 10th overall | |
| **LAGUNA SECA USRRC COMBINED RACE, JUNE 9, 1963** | | | | |
| 196 | Bob Holbert | Shelby Cobra | 4th overall; 1st GT | First USRRC Manufacturer's win |
| 197 | Dave MacDonald | Shelby Cobra | 7th overall; 2nd GT | |
| 198 | Ken Miles | Shelby Cobra | 9th overall; 4th GT | |
| **LE MANS 24-HOUR RACE, JUNE 15 and 16, 1963** | | | | |
| 3 | Peter Bolton/Ninian Sanderson | Shelby Cobra | 7th overall; 3rd GT | |
| 4 | Ed Hugus/Peter Jopp | Shelby Cobra | DNF | |
| **WATKINS GLEN USRRC MANUFACTURER'S RACE, JUNE 30, 1963** | | | | |
| 33 | Bob Johnson | Shelby Cobra | 1st overall | |
| 98 | Ken Miles | Shelby Cobra | 2nd overall | |
| 97 | Dave MacDonald | Shelby Cobra | 3rd overall | |
| 41 | Bob Brown | Shelby Cobra | 5th overall | |
| 54 | Eppie Weitzes | Shelby Cobra | DNF | |
| 99 | Bob Holbert | Shelby Cobra | DNF | |
| **WATKINS GLEN USRRC DRIVER'S CHAMPIONSHIP RACE, JUNE 30, 1963** | | | | |
| 98 | Ken Miles | Shelby Cobra | 3rd overall | |

## KENT USRRC MANUFACTURER'S RACE, JULY 21, 1963
| 97 | Dave MacDonald | Shelby Cobra | 1st overall |
| 98 | Ken Miles | Shelby Cobra | 2nd overall |
| 99 | Bob Holbert | Shelby Cobra | 3rd overall |

## KENT USRRC DRIVER'S RACE, JULY 21, 1963
| 99 | Bob Holbert | Shelby Cobra | 4th overall |
| 98 | Ken Miles | Shelby Cobra | 5th overall |
| 97 | Dave MacDonald | Shelby Cobra | 6th overall |

## GUARDS' INTERNATIONAL TROPHY—BRANDS HATCH, AUGUST 6, 1963
| 17 | Peter Jopp | Shelby Cobra | DNS |

## CONTINENTAL DIVIDE USRRC COMBINED RACE, AUGUST 18, 1963.
| 99 | Bob Holbert | Shelby Cobra | 2nd overall, 2nd Driver's Championship |
| 98 | Bob Bondurant | Shelby Cobra | 5th overall, 1st GT |
| 97 | Dave MacDonald | Shelby Cobra | 8th overall, 2nd GT |
| 45 | R. E. L. Hayes | Shelby Cobra | 9th overall, 3rd GT |

## RAC TOURIST TROPHY—GOODWOOD, AUGUST 24, 1963
| 3 | Bob Olthoff | Shelby Cobra | DNS problems | Homologation |
| 4 | Ken Miles | Shelby Cobra | DNS problems | Homologation |

## ROAD AMERICA 500 USRRC RACE, SEPTEMBER 8, 1963
| 98 | Bob Holbert/Ken Miles | Shelby Cobra | 2nd overall |
| 97 | Dave MacDonald/Bob Bondurant | Shelby Cobra | 4th overall, 1st GT |
| 99 | Lew Spencer/Bob Johnson | Shelby Cobra | 6th overall, 2nd GT |
| 13 | Tom Payne/Dan Gerber | Shelby Cobra | 38th overall, 5th GT |

## BRIDGEHAMPTON 500, SEPTEMBER 14, 1963
| 97 | Dan Gurney | Shelby Cobra | 1st overall | 1st FIA win by an American car |
| 98 | Ken Miles | Shelby Cobra | 2nd overall |
| 99 | Bob Holbert | Shelby Cobra | DNF |
| 33 | Bob Johnson | Shelby Cobra | DNF |
| 41 | Bob Brown | Shelby Cobra | DNF |

## MANSFIELD, OHIO, USRRC MANUFACTURER'S RACE, SEPTEMBER 22, 1963
| 99 | Bob Holbert | Shelby Cobra | 1st overall |
| 98 | Ken Miles | Shelby Cobra | 2nd overall; also won Driver's Race |

## NORTHWEST GRAND PRIX—KENT, SEPTEMBER 27, 1963
| 98 | Dave MacDonald | Shelby King Cobra | DNF |
| 99 | Bob Holbert | Shelby King Cobra | DNF |

## CANADIAN SPORTS CAR GRAND PRIX—MOSPORT, SEPTEMBER 28, 1963
| 54 | Eppie Weitzes | Shelby Cobra | 6th overall, 1st GT |
| 50 | Ken Miles | Shelby Cobra | 7th overall, 2nd GT |
| 33 | Bob Johnson | Shelby Cobra | DNF |

## L.A. TIMES 1-HOUR GT RACE—RIVERSIDE, OCTOBER 13, 1963
| 99 | Bob Bondurant | Shelby Cobra | 1st overall |
| 96 | Allen Grant | Shelby Cobra | 2nd overall |
| 98 | Lew Spencer | Shelby Cobra | 3rd overall |
| 97 | Dan Gurney | Shelby Cobra | 4th overall |
| 37 | Paul Cunningham | Shelby Cobra | DNF |

## L.A. TIMES GRAND PRIX—RIVERSIDE, OCTOBER 13, 1963
| 98 | Dave MacDonald | Shelby King Cobra | 1st overall |
| 299 | Bob Bondurant | Shelby Cobra | 8th overall |
| 99 | Bob Holbert | Shelby King Cobra | DNF |

## MONTEREY GRAND PRIX—LAGUNA SECA, OCTOBER 18, 1963

| 98 | Dave MacDonald | Shelby King Cobra | 1st overall | Also won two A |
| 96 | Allen Grant | Shelby Cobra | 8th overall | Production races |
| 99 | Bob Holbert | Shelby King Cobra | DNF | |

## SOUTH AFRICAN 9-HOUR RACE—KYALAMI, NOVEMBER 2, 1963

| 2 | Bob Olthoff/Frank Gardner | Shelby Cobra | 2nd overall |

## TOUR DE CORSE—CORSICA, NOVEMBER 9 & 10, 1963

| 85 | Jo Schlesser/Patrick Vanson | Shelby Cobra | Finish unknown |

## NASSAU TOURIST TROPHY RACE, DECEMBER 1, 1963

| 106 | John Everly | Shelby Cobra | DNF |
| 98 | Bob Holbert | Shelby Cobra | DNF |
| 45 | George Butler | Shelby Cobra | DNF |

## NASSAU GOVERNOR'S TROPHY RACE, DECEMBER 6, 1963

| 49 | George Butler | Shelby Cobra | 11th overall |
| 98 | Frank Gardner | Shelby Cobra | 12th overall |
| 97 | Dave MacDonald | Shelby King Cobra | DNF |

## NASSAU TROPHY RACE, DECEMBER 8, 1963

| 198 | Frank Gardner | Shelby Cobra | 7th overall |
| 49 | George Butler | Shelby Cobra | 13th overall |
| 106 | John Everly | Shelby Cobra | 16th overall |
| 97 | Dave MacDonald | Shelby King Cobra | DNF |
| 197 | Ken Miles | Shelby Cobra | DNF |
| 98 | Bob Holbert | Shelby King Cobra | DNF |

## DAYTONA CONTINENTAL 2,000-km RACE, FEBRUARY 16, 1964

| 16 | Dan Gurney/Bob Johnson | Shelby Cobra | 4th overall |
| 10 | Ed Butler/Charlie Rainville | Shelby Cobra | 7th overall |
| 18 | Tommy Hitchcock/Zourab Tchkotoura | Shelby Cobra | 10th overall |
| 14 | Dave MacDonald/Bob Holbert | Shelby Daytona Cobra Coupe | DNF |
| 20 | Jeff Stevens/Ralph Noseda | Shelby Cobra | DNF |
| 24 | Graham Shaw/Charlie Hayes/Ed Rahal | Shelby Cobra | DNF |
| 15 | Jo Schlesser/Jean Guichet | Shelby Cobra | DNF |
| 11 | John Everly/Johnny Allen | Shelby Cobra | DNF |

## AUGUSTA USRRC MANUFACTURER'S RACE, MARCH 1, 1964

| 15 | Ken Miles | Shelby Cobra | 1st overall |
| 16 | Dave MacDonald | Shelby Cobra | 2nd overall |
| 20 | Ralph Nosedo/Jeff Stevens | Shelby Cobra | 3rd overall |
| 24 | Graham Shaw | Shelby Cobra | DNF |

## AUGUSTA USSRC DRIVER'S RACE, MARCH 1, 1964

| 97 | Dave MacDonald | Shelby King Cobra | 1st overall |
| 98 | Bob Holbert | Shelby King Cobra | 3rd overall |
| 15 | Ken Miles | Shelby Cobra | 6th overall |

## SEBRING 12-HOUR RACE, MARCH 21, 1964

| 10 | Dave MacDonald/Bob Holbert | Shelby Daytona Cobra Coupe | 4th overall, 1st GT |
| 12 | Lew Spencer/Bob Bondurant | Shelby Cobra | 5th overall, 2nd GT |
| 14 | Jo Schlesser/Phil Hill | Shelby Cobra | 6th overall, 3rd GT |
| 80 | Skip Scott/Hal Keck | Shelby Cobra | 8th overall, 5th GT |
| 15 | Tommy Hitchcock/Zourab Tchkotoura | Shelby Cobra | 14th overall, 10th GT |
| 18 | Ed Lowther/George Wintersteen | Shelby Cobra | 35th overall |
| 16 | Jeff Srevens/Ralph Noseda | Shelby Cobra | 42nd overall |
| 19 | George Reed/Dan Gerber | Shelby Cobra | 43rd overall |
| 1 | Ken Miles/John Morton | Shelby Cobra 427 Prototype | 47th overall, DNF |
| 17 | Charlie Hayes/Tiny Lund/Graham Shaw | Shelby Cobra | 50th overall, DNF |

## PENSACOLA USRRC MANUFACTURER'S CHAMPIONSHIP RACE, APRIL 5, 1964

| 14 | Ken Miles | Shelby Cobra | 1st overall |
| 15 | Graham Shaw | Shelby Cobra | 2nd overall |
| 8 | Ralph Noseda | Shelby Cobra | 3rd overall |

## PENSACOLA USSRC DRIVER'S CHAMPIONSHIP RACE, APRIL 5, 1964

| 98 | Ken Miles | Shelby King Cobra | DNF |
| 97 | Bob Holbert | Shelby King Cobra | DNF |
| 8 | Jeff Stevens | Shelby Cobra | 8th overall |

## PHOENIX FIA OPEN RACE, APRIL 19, 1964
| | | | |
|---|---|---|---|
| 97 | Dave MacDonald | Lang Cooper | 1st overall |
| 15 | Ken Miles | Shelby Cobra | 7th overall, 1st GT |
| 86 | Fito Hafner | Shelby Cobra | 1st in A Production Race |

## TARGA FLORIO, APRIL 26, 1964
| | | | |
|---|---|---|---|
| 146 | Dan Gurney/Jerry Grant | Shelby Cobra | 8th overall, 7th GT |
| 142 | Phil Hill/Bob Bondurant | Shelby Cobra | DNF |
| 148 | Innes Ireland/Masten Gregory | Shelby Cobra | DNF |
| 151 | Enzo Arena/Vito Coco | Shelby Cobra | DNF |
| 152 | Tommy Hitchcock/Zourab Tchkotoura | Shelby Cobra | DNF |

## RIVERSIDE USRRC MANUFACTURER'S RACE, APRIL 26, 1964
| | | | |
|---|---|---|---|
| 50 | Ken Miles | Shelby Cobra | 1st overall |
| 98 | Ed Leslie | Shelby Cobra | 2nd overall |

## RIVERSIDE USRRC DRIVER'S CHAMPIONSHIP RACE, APRIL 26, 1964
| | | | |
|---|---|---|---|
| 97 | Dave MacDonald | Lang Cooper | DNF |
| 98 | Bob Holbert | Shelby King Cobra | DNF |

## LAGUNA SECA USRRC MANUFACTURER'S RACE, MAY 3, 1964
| | | | |
|---|---|---|---|
| 98 | Ed Leslie | Shelby Cobra | 1st overall |
| 50 | Ken Miles | Shelby Cobra | 2nd overall |
| 33 | Bob Johnson | Shelby Cobra | 3rd overall |

## LAGUNA SECA USRRC DRIVER'S CHAMPIONSHIP RACE, MAY 3, 1964
| | | | |
|---|---|---|---|
| 97 | Dave MacDonald | Lang Cooper | 2nd overall |
| 98 | Ed Leslie | Shelby Cobra | 5th overall |
| 114 | Bob Holbert | Shelby King Cobra | DNF |

## KENT USRRC MANUFACTURER'S RACE, MAY 10, 1964
| | | | |
|---|---|---|---|
| 50 | Ken Miles | Shelby Cobra | 1st overall |
| 98 | Ed Leslie | Shelby Cobra | 2nd overall |
| 33 | Bob Johnson | Shelby Cobra | 3rd overall |
| ?? | John Razelle | Shelby Cobra | 9th overall |

## KENT USRRC DRIVER'S CHAMPIONSHIP RACE, MAY 10, 1964
| | | | |
|---|---|---|---|
| 14 | Dave MacDonald | Shelby King Cobra | 1st overall |
| 50 | Ken Miles | Shelby Cobra | 4th overall |
| 98 | Ed Leslie | Shelby Cobra | DNF |
| ?? | John Razelle | Shelby Cobra | DNF |
| 97 | Bob Holbert | Lang Cooper | DNS; practice crash |

## 500-km OF SPA FRANCORCHAMPS, MAY 17, 1964
| | | | |
|---|---|---|---|
| 3 | Bob Bondurant | Shelby Cobra | 9th overall |
| 1 | Phil Hill | Shelby Daytona Cobra Coupe | Finish unkown |
| 4 | Jochen Neerpasch | Shelby Cobra | 11th overall |
| 2 | Innes Ireland | Shelby Cobra | 15th overall |

## ADAC 1,000-km RENNEN NÜRBURGRING, MAY 31, 1964
| | | | |
|---|---|---|---|
| 99 | Jo Schlesser/Richard Attwood | Shelby Cobra | 23rd overall, |
| 96 | Paul Hawkins/Bob Olthoff | Shelby Cobra | 47th overall; DNF |
| 101 | Bob Bondurant/Jochen Neerpasch | Shelby Cobra | DNF |
| 95 | Tommy Hitchcock/Thiel | Shelby Cobra | DNF |
| 100 | Enzo Arena/Vito Coco | Shelby Cobra | DNS; practice crash |

## PLAYER'S 200–MOSPORT, JUNE 6, 1964
| | | | |
|---|---|---|---|
| 14 | Augie Pabst | Shelby King Cobra | 2nd overall |
| 55 | Ludwig Heimrath | Shelby King Cobra | 4th overall |
| 33 | Bob Johnson | Shelby Cobra | 8th overall, 1st GT |
| 119 | Dan Gerber | Shelby Cobra | 14th overall |
| 50 | Ken Miles | Shelby Cobra | DNS; blown engine |

## LE MANS 24-HOUR RACE, JUNE 21 and 22, 1964
| | | | |
|---|---|---|---|
| 5 | Dan Gurney/Bob Bondurant | Shelby Daytona Cobra Coupe | 4th overall, 1st GT |
| 64 | Regis Fraissinet/Jean deMortemart | Shelby Cobra | 18th overall |
| 6 | Chris Amon/Jochen Neerpasch | Shelby Daytona Cobra Coupe | Disqualfied |
| 3 | Jack Sears/Peter Bolton | AC Cobra Coupe | DNF |

## WATKINS GLEN USRRC MANUFACTURER'S RACE, JUNE 28, 1964
| | | | |
|---|---|---|---|
| 98 | Ken Miles | Shelby Cobra | 1st overall |
| 99 | Ed Leslie | Shelby Cobra | 2nd overall |
| 33 | Bob Johnson | Shelby Cobra | 3rd overall |
| 44 | Graham Shaw | Shelby Cobra | 4th overall |
| 88 | Hal Keck | Shelby Cobra | 5th overall |

## WATKINS GLEN USRRC DRIVER'S CHAMPIONSHIP RACE, JUNE 28, 1964

| 55 | Ludwig Heimrath | Shelby King Cobra | 4th overall |
| 98 | Ken Miles | Shelby Cobra | 5th overall |
| 33 | Bob Johnson | Shelby Cobra | 8th overall |

## REIMS 12-HOUR RACE, JULY 4 and 5, 1964

| 14 | Innes Ireland/Jochen Neerpasch | Shelby Daytona Cobra Coupe | DNF |
| 15 | Dan Gurney/Bob Bondurant | Shelby Daytona Cobra Coupe | DNF |

## ILFORD FILMS TROPHY—BRANDS HATCH, JULY 11, 1964

| 32 | Jack Sears | Shelby Cobra | 1st overall |
| 26 | Roy Salvadori | Shelby Cobra | 3rd overall |
| 34 | Bob Olthoff | Shelby Cobra | DNS; practice crash |

## GREENWOOD USRRC COMBINED RACE, JULY 19, 1964

| 96 | Ed Leslie | Shelby King Cobra | 1st overall |
| 98 | Ken Miles | Shelby Cobra | 4th overall, 1st GT |
| 19 | Dan Gerber | Shelby Cobra | 5th overall, 2nd GT |
| 10 | Hal Keck | Shelby Cobra | 3nd GT |
| 33 | Bob Johnson | Shelby Cobra | DNF |

## GUARDS' INTERNATIONAL TROPHY—BRANDS HATCH, AUGUST 3, 1964

| 26 | Jack Sears | Shelby Cobra | 5th overall, 1st GT |
| 25 | Chris Amon | Shelby Cobra | 6th overall, 2nd GT |
| 34 | Tommy Hitchcock | Shelby Cobra | 15th overall |
| 27 | Bob Olthoff | Shelby Cobra | 16th overall |

## FREIBURG-SCHAUINSLAND HILLCLIMB, AUGUST 8, 1964

| 66 | Bob Bondurant | Shelby Cobra | 4th overall, 1st GT |
| 68 | Jochen Neerpasch | Shelby Cobra | 9th overall, 3rd GT |
| 67 | Jo Siffert | Shelby Cobra | 16th overall, 4th GT |

## MEADOWDALE USRRC MANUFACTURER'S RACE, AUGUST 9, 1964

| 98 | Ken Miles | Shelby Cobra | 1st overall |
| 99 | Bob Johnson | Shelby Cobra | 2nd overall |
| 13 | Tom Payne | Shelby Cobra | 3rd overall |
| 44 | Jerry Hansen | Shelby Cobra | 4th overall |

## MEADOWDALE USRRC DRIVER'S RACE, AUGUST 9, 1964

| 98 | Ken Miles | Shelby Cobra | 5th overall |
| 96 | Ed Leslie | Shelby King Cobra | DNF |

## RAC TOURIST TROPHY–GOODWOOD, AUGUST 29, 1964

| 21 | Dan Gurney | Shelby Daytona Cobra Coupe | 3rd overall, 1st GT |
| 23 | Jack Sears | Shelby Cobra | 4th overall, 2nd GT |
| 24 | Bob Olthoff | Shelby Cobra | 5th overall, 3rd GT |
| 22 | Phil Hill | Shelby Daytona Cobra Coupe | 11th overall |
| 25 | Roy Salvadori | Shelby Cobra | DNF |

## SIERRE-MONTANA HILLCLIMB, AUGUST 30, 1964

| 176 | Bob Bondurant | Shelby Cobra | 5th overall, 1st GT |
| 177 | Jo Schlesser | Shelby Cobra | 8th overall, 2nd GT |
| 175 | Jochen Neerpasch | Shelby Cobra | 11th overall, 4th GT |

## TOUR DE FRANCE, SEPTEMBER 11–20, 1964

| 185 | Guy Ligier/Henri Morrogh | Shelby Daytona Coupe | DNS | |
| 186 | Andre Simon/Maurice Dupeyron | Shelby Daytona Cobra Coupe | | DNF |
| 187 | Bob Bondurant/Jochen Neerpasch | Shelby Daytona Cobra Coupe | | DNF |
| 188 | Maurice Trintignant/Bernard de St. Auban | Shelby Daytona Coupe | DNF | |
| 189 | Jean Vincent/Gerard Faget | Shelby Cobra | | DNF |

## ROAD AMERICA 500 USRRC RACE, SEPTEMBER 13, 1964

| 97 | Ken Miles/Skip Scott/John Morton | Shelby Cobra | 2nd overall, 1st GT |
| 89 | Pete Harrison/Art Huttinger | Shelby Cobra | 26th overall |
| 98 | Ronnie Bucknum/Ken Miles | Shelby Cobra | 28th overall |
| 65 | Pat Manning/Bob Liess | Shelby Cobra | 32nd overall |
| 99 | Bob Johnson/Ed Leslie | Shelby Cobra | DNF |
| 32 | John Everly | Shelby Cobra | DNF |

## BRIDGEHAMPTON 500, SEPTEMBER 20, 1964

| 98 | Ken Miles | Shelby Cobra | 4th overall, 1st GT |
|----|-----------|--------------|---------------------|
| 97 | Ronnie Bucknum | Shelby Cobra | 6th overall, 2nd GT |
| 96 | Bob Johnson | Shelby Cobra | 7th overall, 3rd GT |
| 60 | Chuck Parsons | Shelby Cobra | 8th overall, 4th GT |
| 65 | Art Huttinger/Pete Harrison | Shelby Cobra | 9th overall, 5th GT |
| 94 | Joe Freites/John Morton | Shelby Cobra | 11th overall, 6th GT |
| 99 | Ed Leslie | Shelby Cobra | DNF |
| 66 | Lew Florence | Shelby Cobra | DNF |
| 95 | Charlie Hayes | Shelby Cobra | DNF |
| 62 | Hal Keck | Shelby Cobra | DNF |

## CANADIAN SPORTS CAR GRAND PRIX—MOSPORT, SEPTEMBER 26, 1964

| 55 | Ludwig Heimrath | Shelby King Cobra | 6th overall |
|----|-----------------|-------------------|-------------|
| 83 | Jean Ouellet | Shelby Cobra | 1st overall, FIA Production Car race |

## L.A. TIMES THREE-HOUR ENDURO—RIVERSIDE, OCTOBER 10, 1964

| 45 | Lew Spencer | Shelby Cobra | 5th overall |
|----|-------------|--------------|-------------|

## L.A. TIMES GRAND PRIX—RIVERSIDE, OCTOBER 11, 1964

| 94 | Parnelli Jones | Shelby King Cobra | 1st overall |
|----|----------------|-------------------|-------------|
| 97 | Ed Leslie | Lang Cooper | 4th overall |
| 93 | Bob Bondurant | Shelby King Cobra | 5th overall |
| 92 | Richie Ginther | Shelby King Cobra | 7th overall |
| 95 | Ronnie Bucknum | Shelby King Cobra | DNF |
| 98 | Ken Miles | Shelby Cobra | DNF |

## MONTEREY GRAND PRIX—LAGUNA SECA, OCTOBER 18, 1964

| 96 | Bob Bondurant | Shelby King Cobra | 3rd overall |
|----|---------------|-------------------|-------------|
| 97 | Ed Leslie | Shelby King Cobra | 5th overall |
| 195 | Ronnie Bucknum | Shelby King Cobra | 6th overall |
| 98 | Parnelli Jones | Shelby King Cobra | DNF |

## SOUTH AFRICAN 9-HOUR RACE—KYALAMI, OCTOBER 21, 1964

| 8 | Jack Sears/Bob Olthoff | Willment Cobra Coupe | 5th overall |
|---|------------------------|----------------------|-------------|

## NASSAU TOURIST TROPHY, NOVEMBER 29, 1964

| 92 | Bob Johnson | Shelby Cobra | 4th overall |
|----|-------------|--------------|-------------|
| 73 | Tom Payne | Shelby Cobra | 5th overall |
| 98 | Ken Miles | Shelby 390 Cobra Prototype | DNF |
| 89 | Hans Schenk | Shelby Cobra | DNF |
| 19 | Dan Gerber | Shelby Cobra | DNF |
| 103 | Ralph Noseda | Shelby Cobra | DNF |

## NASSAU GOVERNOR'S TROPHY, DECEMBER 4, 1964

| 73 | Tom Payne | Shelby Cobra | 9th overall |
|----|-----------|--------------|-------------|
| 103 | Ralph Noseda | Shelby Cobra | DNF |

## NASSAU TROPHY RACE, DECEMBER 6, 1964

| 155 | Ludwig Heimrath | Shelby King Cobra | 7th overall |
|-----|-----------------|-------------------|-------------|
| 73 | Tom Payne | Shelby Cobra | 25th overall |
| 103 | Ralph Noseda | Shelby Cobra | 32nd overall |
| 98 | Ken Miles | Shelby 390 Cobra Prototype | DNF |
| 92 | Bob Johnson | Shelby Cobra | DNF |
| 19 | Dan Gerber | Shelby Cobra | DNF |

## DAYTONA CONTINENTAL 2,000-km RACE, FEBRUARY 28, 1965

| 73 | Ken Miles/Lloyd Ruby | Shelby Ford GT40 | 1st overall |
|----|----------------------|------------------|-------------|
| 13 | Jo Schlesser/Hal Keck | Shelby Daytona Cobra Coupe | 2nd overall, 1st GT |
| 72 | Bob Bondurant/Richie Ginther | Shelby Ford GT40 | 3rd overall |
| 14 | John Timanus/Rick Muther | Shelby Daytona Cobra Coupe | 4th overall, 2nd GT |
| 11 | Ed Leslie/Allen Grant | Shelby Daytona Cobra Coupe | 6th overall, 4th GT |
| 36 | Graham Shaw/Dick Thompson | Shelby Cobra | 10th overall, 8th GT |
| 19 | Pete Harrison/Lin Coleman | Shelby Cobra | DNF |
| 12 | Bob Johnson/Tom Payne | Shelby Daytona Cobra Coupe | DNF |

## SEBRING 12-HOUR RACE, MARCH 27, 1965

| 11 | Bruce McLaren/Ken Miles | Shelby Ford GT40 | 2nd overall |
|----|-------------------------|------------------|-------------|
| 15 | Jo Schlesser/Bob Bondurant | Shelby Daytona Cobra Coupe | 4th overall, 1st GT |
| 14 | Bob Johnson/Tom Payne | Shelby Daytona Cobra Coupe | 7th overall, 4th GT |
| 12 | Ed Leslie/Allen Grant | Shelby Daytona Cobra Coupe | 13th overall, 6th GT |
| 17 | Graham Shaw/Dick Thompson | Shelby Cobra | 19th overall, 9th GT |
| 16 | Jim Adams/Phil Hill | Shelby Daytona Cobra Coupe | 21st overall |
| 18 | Ed Lowther/Bob Nagel | Shelby Cobra | DNF |
| 20 | George Reed/Dan Gerber | Shelby Cobra | DNF |
| 10 | Phil Hill/Richie Ginther | Shelby Ford GT40 | DNF |
| 19 | Pete Harrison/Linley Coleman | Shelby Cobra | DNS |

## PENSACOLA USRRC DRIVER'S AND MANUFACTURER'S RACE, APRIL 11, 1965

| 91 | Skip Scott | Shelby Cobra 427 | 3rd overall |
|----|------------|------------------|-------------|
| 13 | Tom Payne | Shelby Cobra | 6th overall, 1st GT |
| 98 | Bob Johnson | Shelby Cobra | 13th overall, 4th GT |

## 1,000-km OF MONZA, APRIL 25, 1965

| 69 | Bruce McLaren/Ken Miles | Shelby Ford GT40 | 5th overall |
|----|-------------------------|------------------|-------------|
| 48 | Bob Bondurant/Allen Grant | Shelby Daytona Cobra Coupe | 7th overall, 1st GT |
| 49 | Jack Sears/John Whitmore | Shelby Daytona Cobra Coupe | 11th overall, 2nd GT |
| 52 | John Sparrow/N. A. Dangerfield | Shelby Cobra | 12th overall |
| 68 | Chris Amon/Umberto Maglioli | Shelby Ford GT40 | DNF |
| 51 | Chris McLaren/Harry Digby | Shelby Cobra | DNF |

## RAC TOURIST TROPHY—OULTON PARK, MAY 1, 1965

| 21 | John Whitmore | Shelby Cobra | 4th overall, 1st GT |
|----|---------------|--------------|---------------------|
| 25 | Allen Grant | Shelby Cobra | 6th overall, 3rd GT |
| 22 | Jack Sears | Shelby Daytona Cobra Coupe | 7th overall, 4th GT |
| 28 | John Sparrow | Shelby Cobra | 8th overall, 5th GT |
| 23 | Frank Gardner | Willment Cobra Coupe | 10th overall, 6th GT |
| 26 | N. A. Dangerfield | Shelby Cobra | DNF |
| 24 | Roger Mac | Shelby Cobra | DNF |

## RIVERSIDE USRRC MANUFACTURER'S RACE, MAY 2, 1965

| 98 | Ken Miles | Shelby Cobra | 1st overall |
|----|-----------|--------------|-------------|
| 97 | Bob Johnson | Shelby Cobra | 3rd overall |
| 96 | Ed Leslie | Shelby Cobra | DNF |
| 11 | Ernie Kesling | Shelby Cobra | DNF |
| 2 | Lothar Motschenbacher | Shelby Cobra | DNF |

## RIVERSIDE USRRC DRIVER'S CHAMPIONSHIP RACE, MAY 2, 1965

| 98 | Ken Miles | Shelby Cobra 427 Prototype | DNF |
|----|-----------|----------------------------|-----|
| 1 | Lothar Motschenbacher | Cobra 427 | DNF |

## TARGA FLORIO, MAY 9, 1965

| 194 | John Whitmore/Bob Bondurant | Shelby Ford GT40 | DNF |
|-----|-----------------------------|------------------|-----|

## LAGUNA SECA USRRC MANUFACTURER'S RACE, MAY 9, 1965

| 98 | Ken Miles | Shelby Cobra | 1st overall |
|----|-----------|--------------|-------------|
| 96 | Ed Leslie | Shelby Cobra | 2nd overall |
| 47 | Foster Alexander | Shelby Cobra | 15th overall |
| 96 | Bob Johnson | Shelby Cobra | 16th overall |
| 1 | Ernie Kesling | Shelby Cobra | DNF |

## LAGUNA SECA USRRC DRIVER'S CHAMPIONSHIP RACE, MAY 9, 1965

| 1 | Lothar Motschenbacher | Shelby Cobra 427 | 7th overall |
|---|-----------------------|------------------|-------------|

## 500 km OF SPA FRANCORCHAMPS, MAY 16, 1965

| 20 | Bob Bondurant | Shelby Daytona Cobra Coupe | 5th overall, 3rd GT |
|----|---------------|----------------------------|---------------------|
| 23 | Chris McLaren | Shelby Cobra | Finish position unknown |
| 26 | Nick Granville-Smith | Shelby Cobra | Finish position unknown |
| 21 | John Whitmore | Shelby Daytona Cobra Coupe | DNF |
| 22 | Harry Digby | Shelby Cobra | DNF |

## ADAC 1,000 km RENNEN NÜRBURGRING, MAY 23, 1965

| 54 | Bob Bondurant/Jochen Neerpasch | Shelby Daytona Cobra Coupe | 7th overall, 1st GT |
|----|--------------------------------|----------------------------|---------------------|
| 11 | Ronnie Bucknum/Chris Amon/Phil Hill | Shelby Ford GT40 | 8th overall |
| 55 | Jack Sears/Frank Gardner | Shelby Daytona Cobra Coupe | 10th overall, 2nd GT |
| 56 | Andre Simon/Jo Schlesser | Shelby Cobra Daytona Coupe | 12 overall, 4th GT |
| 52 | Chris McLaren/John Sparrow | Shelby Cobra | DNF |
| 12 | Phil Hill/Bruce McLaren | Shelby Ford GT40 | DNF |

## BRIDGEHAMPTON USRRC COMBINED RACE, MAY 23, 1965
| 91 | Skip Scott | Shelby Cobra 427 | 5th overall |
| 33 | Bob Johnson | Shelby Cobra | 7th overall, 1st GT |
| 13 | Tom Payne | Shelby Cobra | 10th overall, 2nd GT |
| ?? | Ray Cuomo | Shelby Cobra | 11th overall, 3rd GT |

## PLAYER'S 200–MOSPORT, JUNE 5, 1965
| 33 | Bob Johnson | Shelby Cobra | 4th overall |
| 113 | Tom Payne | Shelby Cobra | DNF |

## ROSSFELD BERGRENNEN HILLCLIMB, JUNE 13, 1965
| 21 | Bob Bondurant | Shelby Cobra | 10th overall, 1st GT |
| 22 | Bo Ljungfeldt | Shelby Cobra | Unknown finish |

## LE MANS 24-HOUR RACE, JUNE 19 AND 20, 1965
| 11 | Jack Sears/Dick Thompson | Shelby Daytona Cobra Coupe | 7th overall, 3rd GT |
| 9 | Dan Gurney/Jerry Grant | Shelby Daytona Cobra Coupe | DNF |
| 10 | Bob Johnson/Tom Payne | Shelby Daytona Cobra Coupe | DNF |
| 12 | Jo Schlesser/Allen Grant | Shelby Daytona Cobra Coupe | DNF |
| 59 | Peter Sutcliffe/Peter Harper | Shelby Daytona Cobra Coupe | DNF |
| 15 | Maurice Trintignant/Guy Ligier | Shelby Ford GT40 | DNF |
| 14 | Innes Ireland/John Whitmore | Shelby Ford GT40 | DNF |
| 6 | Ronnie Bucknum/Herbert Muller | Shelby Ford GT40 | DNF |
| 7 | Bob Bondurant/Umberto Maglioli | Shelby Ford GT40 | DNF |
| 1 | Ken Miles/Bruce McLaren | Shelby Ford Mk. II | DNF |
| 2 | Phil Hill/Chris Amon | Shelby Ford Mk. II | DNF |

## WATKINS GLEN USRRC COMBINED RACE, JUNE 27, 1965
| 91 | Skip Scott | Shelby Cobra 427 | 3rd overall |
| 33 | Bob Johnson | Shelby Cobra | 6th overall, 1st GT |
| 88 | Hal Keck | Shelby Cobra | 17th overall, 3rd GT |
| 13 | Tom Payne | Shelby Cobra | DNF |

## 12 HOURS OF REIMS, JULY 4, 1965
| 26 | Bob Bondurant/Jo Schlesser | Shelby Daytona Cobra Coupe | 5th overall, 1st GT |
| 27 | Jack Sears/John Whitmore | Shelby Daytona Cobra Coupe | 9th overall, 3rd GT |
| 25 | Frank Gardner/Innes Ireland | Willment Cobra Coupe | DNF |

## KENT USRRC COMBINED RACE, AUGUST 1, 1965
| 13 | Tom Payne | Shelby Cobra | 1st GT |
| 44 | Lew Florence | Shelby Cobra | 2nd GT |
| 33 | Bob Johnson | Shelby Cobra | 3rd GT |

## COPPA DI ENNA, AUGUST 15, 1965
| 23 | Bob Bondurant | Shelby Daytona Cobra Coupe | 3rd overall, 1st GT |
| 20 | Jack Sears | Shelby Daytona Cobra Coupe | 4th overall, 2nd GT |

## CONTINENTAL DIVIDE USRRC COMBINED RACE, AUGUST 15, 1965
| 91 | Skip Scott | Shelby Cobra 427 | 6th overall |
| 33 | Bob Johnson | Shelby Cobra | 7th overall, 1st GT |
| 13 | Tom Payne | Shelby Cobra | 12th overall, 4th GT |
| 19 | Dan Gerber | Shelby Cobra | 13th overall, 5th GT |

## MID-OHIO USRRC COMBINED RACE, AUGUST 29, 1965
| 19 | Dan Gerber | Shelby Cobra | 8th overall, 1st GT |
| 13 | Tom Payne | Shelby Cobra | 9th overall, 2nd GT |
| 33 | Bob Johnson | Shelby Cobra | DNF |

## ROAD AMERICA 500 USRRC RACE, SEPTEMBER 5, 1965
| 91 | Dick Thompson/Ed Lowther | Shelby Cobra 427 | 3rd overall |
| 13 | Tom Payne/Ray Cuomo | Shelby Cobra | 7th overall, 1st GT |
| 33 | Bob Johnson/Don Sesslar | Shelby Cobra | 13th overall, 2nd GT |
| 19 | Dan Gerber/Tom Yeager | Shelby Cobra | 33rd overall |

## PLAYER'S QUEBEC—ST. JOVITE, SEPTEMBER 19, 1965
| 13 | Tom Payne | Shelby Cobra | 7th overall, 1st in FIA Production Race |
| 19 | Dan Gerber | Shelby Cobra | 9th overall, 2nd in FIA Production Race |
| 324 | Larry Cohen | Shelby Cobra | DNS, 5th in FIA Production Race |
| 83 | Jean Ouellet | Shelby Cobra | DNS, 7th in FIA Production Race |

## BRIDGEHAMPTON 500, SEPTEMBER 19, 1965

| | | | |
|---|---|---|---|
| 91 | Skip Scott/Dick Thompson | Shelby Cobra 427 | 3rd overall |
| 33 | Bob Johnson | Shelby Cobra | 5th overall, 1st GT |
| 13 | Ray Cuomo | Shelby Cobra | 6th overall, 2nd GT |

## CANADIAN GRAND PRIX FOR SPORTS CARS–MOSPORT, SEPTEMBER 25, 1965

| | | | |
|---|---|---|---|
| 31 | Bob Johnson | Shelby Cobra | 10th overall |
| 13 | Tom Payne | Shelby Cobra | 11th overall |
| 83 | Jean Ouellet | Shelby Cobra | DNF |

## MONTEREY GRAND PRIX—LAGUNA SECA, OCTOBER 17, 1965

| | | | |
|---|---|---|---|
| 91 | Dick Thompson | Shelby Cobra 427 | 10th overall |

## L.A. TIMES ONE-HOUR ENDURO—RIVERSIDE, OCTOBER 30, 1965

| | | | |
|---|---|---|---|
| 98 | Lothar Motschenbacher | Shelby Cobra | 1st overall |
| 45 | Lew Spencer | Shelby Cobra | 2nd overall |
| 27 | Fred Whithead | Shelby Cobra | 7th overall |

## L.A. TIMES GRAND PRIX FOR SPORTS CARS–RIVERSIDE, OCTOBER 31, 1965

| | | | |
|---|---|---|---|
| 91 | Dick Thompson | Shelby Cobra 427 | 15th overall |

## STARDUST GRAND PRIX—LAS VEGAS, NOVEMBER 14, 1965

| | | | |
|---|---|---|---|
| 91 | Ed Lowther | Shelby Cobra 427 | 11th overall |

## NASSAU TOURIST TROPHY, NOVEMBER 28, 1965

| | | | |
|---|---|---|---|
| 11 | Tom Payne | Shelby Cobra | 3rd overall |

## GOVERNOR'S TROPHY RACE, DECEMBER 3, 1965

| | | | |
|---|---|---|---|
| 19 | Dan Gerber | Shelby Cobra | 18th overall |
| 91 | Dick Thompson | Shelby Cobra 427 | DNF |

## NASSAU TROPHY RACE, DECEMBER 5, 1965

| | | | |
|---|---|---|---|
| 11 | Bob Grossman | Shelby Cobra | 5th overall |
| 19 | Dan Gerber | Shelby Cobra | 6th overall |
| 91 | Dick Thompson | Shelby Cobra 427 | DNF |

## DAYTONA CONTINENTAL 24-HOUR, FEBRUARY 5 AND 6, 1966

| | | | |
|---|---|---|---|
| 98 | Ken Miles/Lloyd Ruby | Shelby Ford Mk. II | 1st overall * |
| 97 | Dan Gurney/Jerry Grant | Shelby Ford Mk. II | 2nd overall * |
| 95 | Walt Hansgen/Mark Donohue | H & M Ford Mk. II | 3rd overall * |
| 96 | Bruce McLaren/Chris Amon | Shelby Ford Mk. II | 5th overall * |
| 87 | Ronnie Bucknum/Richie Ginther | H & M Ford Mk. II | DNF * |

## SEBRING 12-HOUR RACE, MARCH 26, 1966

| | | | |
|---|---|---|---|
| 1 | Ken Miles/Lloyd Ruby | Shelby Ford Mk. II X1 Roadster | 1st overall * |
| 3 | Walt Hansgen/Mark Donohue | H & M Ford Mk. II | 2nd overall * |
| 4 | A. J. Foyt/Ronnie Bucknum | H & M Ford Mk. II | 12th overall * |
| 2 | Dan Gurney/Jerry Grant | Shelby Ford Mk. II | Disqualified |

## LE MANS 24-HOUR RACE, JUNE 18 AND 19, 1966

| | | | |
|---|---|---|---|
| 2 | Chris Amon/Bruce McLaren | Shelby Ford Mk. II | 1st overall * |
| 1 | Ken Miles/Denis Hulme | Shelby Ford Mk. II | 2nd overall * |
| 5 | Ronnie Bucknum/Dick Hutcherson | H & M Ford Mk. II | 3rd overall * |
| 3 | Dan Gurney/Jerry Grant | Shelby Ford Mk. II | DNF * |
| 7 | Graham Hill/Brian Muir | Alan Mann Racing Ford Mk. II | DNF * |
| 6 | Mario Andretti/Lucien Bianchi | H & M Ford Mk. II | DNF * |
| 8 | John Whitmore/Frank Gardner | Alan Mann Racing Ford Mk. II | DNF * |
| 4 | Paul Hawkins/Mark Donohue | H & M Ford Mk. II | DNF * |

## DAYTONA CONTINENTAL 24-HOUR RACE, FEBRUARY 4 AND 5, 1967

| | | | |
|---|---|---|---|
| 1 | Bruce McLaren/Lucien Bianchi | Shelby Ford Mk. II | 7th overall |
| 3 | Dan Gurney/Jerry Grant | Shelby Ford Mk. II | DNF |
| 6 | Lloyd Ruby/Denis Hulme | H & M Ford Mk. II | DNF |
| 5 | Mario Andretti/Richie Ginther | H & M Ford Mk. II | DNF |
| 2 | Ronnie Bucknum/Frank Gardner | Shelby Ford Mk. II | DNF |
| 4 | Mark Donohue/Peter Revson | H & M Ford Mk. II | DNF |

## SEBRING 12-HOUR RACE, APRIL 1, 1967

| | | | |
|---|---|---|---|
| 1 | Mario Andretti/Bruce McLaren | Shelby Ford Mk. IV | 1st overall |
| 2 | A. J. Foyt/Lloyd Ruby | H & M Ford Mk. II | 2nd overall |

## LE MANS 24-HOUR RACE, JUNE 10 AND 11, 1967

| | | | |
|---|---|---|---|
| 1 | Dan Gurney/A. J. Foyt | Shelby Ford Mk. IV | 1st overall |
| 2 | Bruce McLaren/Mark Donohue | Shelby Ford Mk. IV | 4th overall |
| 57 | Ronnie Bucknum/Paul Hawkins | Shelby Ford Mk. IIB | DNF |
| 3 | Mario Andretti/Lucien Bianchi | H & M Ford Mk. IV | DNF |
| 5 | Frank Gardner/Roger McCluskey | H & M Ford Mk. IV | DNF |
| 6 | Jo Schlesser/Guy Ligier | Ford of France Ford Mk. IIB | DNF |
| 4 | Lloyd Ruby/Denis Hulme | H & M Ford Mk. IV | DNF |

* All of the Ford Mk. II cars were constructed in the shop of Shelby American. After construction and testing, the various cars were maintained and modified by the teams to which they were assigned.

This list is correct to the best of my knowledge and all of the statistics shown here can be verified by photographs, race records, and race reports. Information on several of the USRRC races has been difficult to obtain because most of those records have either been thrown away or lost. The information on this list has been compiled from a number of sources. My first choice for any project such as this is to use the official company records and race records, if they exist. In this case, I have a number of Shelby American race reports, Ford race reports, and FIA track records. I have also used *AutoSport, Automobile Year, Sports Car Graphic, Autocourse, Carroll Shelby's Racing Cobra, The Cobra Ferrari Wars, Sebring,* and *Sun on the Grid* to verify the information used here. It is interesting to note how many discrepancies appear in all of these sources regarding who finished where and who actually drove the car in the first place. There are also considerable problems in trying to find out what many of the car's actual racing numbers were because most of the sources only listed the order of finish and neglected to list any of the proper race numbers for the competing cars.

I hope that this list will be helpful to those who seeking this type of information. Any additional facts, figures, or dates are sincerely welcome.

# Index